Writing

Skills

Grade 5

FlashKids

Spark Publishing

ISBN-13: 978-1-4114-0482-3
ISBN-10: 1-4114-0482-3

For more information, please visit *www.flashkidsbooks.com*
Please submit changes or report errors to *www.flashkidsbooks.com/errors*

Printed and bound in China

Spark Publishing
120 Fifth Avenue
New York, NY 10011

Dear Parent,

Reading and writing well are essential tools for success in all school subjects. In addition, many states now include writing assessments in their standardized tests. There may be no precise formula for good writing, but through studying samples and practicing different styles, your child will build the skills and versatility to approach any writing assignment with ease and confidence.

Each of the six units in this fun, colorful workbook focuses on a unique type of writing that your fifth-grader may be required to use in school or may wish to pursue in his or her free time. These types include personal narrative, how-to writing, story, comparative writing, descriptive writing, and short report. The first half of each unit reinforces writing aspects such as putting ideas in a sequence, using descriptive details, working with a thesaurus, and using proofreading marks, in addition to providing fun, inspirational writing ideas for your child to explore alone or with a friend. The second half of each unit focuses on a practice paper that exemplifies the writing type. After your child reads the practice paper, he or she will analyze it, prepare a writing plan for his or her own paper, write a first draft, revise it, and, lastly, allow you or a friend to score it.

Here are some helpful suggestions for getting the most out of this workbook:

- Provide a quiet place to work.
- Go over the directions together.
- Encourage your child to do his or her best.
- Check each activity when it is complete.
- Review your child's work together, noting good work as well as points for improvement.

As your child completes the units, help him or her maintain a positive attitude about writing. Provide writing opportunities such as a journal, in which your child can write about things that happen each day and can keep a running list of topics or story ideas for future writing projects. Read your child's stories aloud at bedtime, and display his or her writing in your home.

Most importantly, enjoy this time you spend together. Your child's writing skills will improve even more with your dedication and support!

Proofreading Marks

Use the following symbols to help make proofreading faster.

MARK	MEANING	EXAMPLE
◯	spell correctly	I ⟨liek⟩ dogs. *like*
⊙	add period	They are my favorite kind of pet⊙
?	add question mark	Are you lucky enough to have a dog?
⹀	capitalize	My dog's name is scooter.
℘	take out	He is a great companion for me and my ~~my~~ family.
∧	add	We got Scooter when ∧ was eight weeks old. *he*
/	make lowercase	My U̸ncle came over to take a look at him.
∿	switch	He watched the puppy run in around circles.
∧̦	add comma	"Jack, that dog is a real scooter!" he told me.
⋁ ⋁	add quotation marks	Scooter! That's the perfect name! I said.
¶	indent paragraph	¶ Scooter is my best friend in the whole world. He is not only happy and loving but also the smartest dog in the world. Every morning at six o'clock, he jumps on my bed and wakes me with a bark. Then he brings me my toothbrush.

Table of Contents

UNIT 1: Personal Narrative

HOW MUCH DO YOU KNOW?

Read the paragraph. Then answer the questions.

I planned and prepared a surprise party for my sister Susie. I hired a clown and bought some balloons about a week ahead of time. Three days before the party, I ordered a chocolate cake and borrowed extra plates. I shopped, cleaned, and cooked the day before the party.

The guests hid in the basement. When Susie came in, they jumped out and yelled "Surprise!" Susie laughed and danced around in a circle. We wore polka-dot party hats and played Susie's favorite music. Everyone ate, laughed, and danced.

Some of the guests helped clear the table and wash the dishes. I sat and rested.

1. Who is the narrator of the story?

   _____

2. What does the writer tell about in the first paragraph?

   _____

3. What caused Susie to dance around in a circle?

   _____

4. List two details that tell what happened at the party.

   _____

   _____

Analyzing a Personal Narrative

> **A PERSONAL NARRATIVE**
>
> - is a true story the writer tells about himself or herself
> - is written in the first person
> - reveals a writer's feelings about an event or events
> - usually presents events in time order

Read the personal narrative. Answer the questions that follow.

On Saturday afternoon I went to the new barbershop that opened in our neighborhood. I told the barber how I wanted my hair to be cut. Twenty minutes later I walked out with the Mohawk I had always wanted.

When my mom saw my haircut, she almost fainted. She asked, "Why did you do that to yourself?" I told her that I thought she would think it was an original and interesting hairstyle. She said she thought it was an original and terrible hairstyle.

On Monday my teacher made a funny face when he saw my hair. He said, "I hope that's a wig." He was concerned because I was the prince in the school play. A prince with a Mohawk would look pretty strange.

As it turned out, I had to wear a wig for the play. On opening night the wig fell off. When the people in the audience saw the Mohawk, they laughed.

1. What is the topic of this personal narrative?

_____

2. What does the writer tell about in the first paragraph?

_____

3. What does the writer tell about in the second paragraph?

_____

4. What does the writer tell about in the third paragraph?

_____

5. What does the writer tell about in the fourth paragraph?

_____

Connecting Cause and Effect

TO WRITE A PERSONAL NARRATIVE, GOOD WRITERS
- tell what happened
- tell the causes or the effects of the major events

Read each sentence. Circle the part that tells the cause. Draw a line under the part that tells the effect. If the sentence does not show cause and effect, write *none* on the line.

1. In April 1805 Captain Meriwether Lewis and one of his hunters were hiking in what is now Montana.

   _____

2. Two grizzly bears suddenly appeared, and the men were immediately frightened.

   _____

3. The men fired, and one bear was wounded.

   _____

4. The other bear was not hurt, so it ran away.

   _____

5. The wounded bear was very angry, so it charged Captain Lewis.

   _____

6. Because Lewis still had time to reload, he lived to tell the tale.

   _____

7. In the months that followed, Lewis and Clark saw many grizzly bears.

   _____

8. If you bother or frighten a grizzly, it will attack.

   _____

9. Usually, it goes its own way, and a person avoids trouble.

   _____

10. Because these bears do not climb trees, many people have escaped angry grizzlies.

    _____

Using Details to Explain

> **GOOD WRITERS**
> - include details that give causes and effects
> - give their feelings in response to certain causes

He was already an expert rider.

Slow had jabbed the Crow with his stick.

He had a slow and serious nature.

Slow had acted bravely.

They had won the battle.

The Crow Indians had stolen some Sioux horses.

He no longer seemed so slow and serious.

It was considered braver to push an enemy off a horse than to shoot an arrow from far away.

The numbered sentences below tell about events. After each numbered sentence, write the detail sentence from the box that helps explain that event.

1. When Sitting Bull was a child, he was named Slow.

   _____

2. At the age of ten, Slow was given his own pony.

   _____

3. When Slow was fourteen, he and other Sioux fought some Crow Indians.

   _____

4. Slow was armed only with a stick.

   _____

5. One Crow Indian fell from his horse.

   _____

6. The Sioux held a victory party.

   _____

using a Thesaurus

Good writers use a thesaurus to find synonyms that will make their writing interesting and give it variety.

A. Replace each underlined word or words with words that express the meaning in a more exact and vivid way. You may want to refer to a thesaurus.

1. When Harvey was growing up, his family was <u>very large</u>.
   _____

2. At one time Harvey counted <u>about</u> sixty cousins.
   _____

3. They all lived on a large farm, <u>taking care of</u> animals and crops.
   _____

4. Everyone <u>worked hard</u>. _____

5. In the 1930s the family lost the land they had <u>worked</u> for so long.
   _____

6. <u>Things</u> became very <u>hard</u> for the family. _____

7. Harvey's parents found jobs in the <u>shops</u> in town.
   _____

8. Harvey, an <u>ambitious</u> young man, decided that he would have his own store someday. _____

9. <u>Thirty years</u> later, Harvey owned one of the largest chains of stores in the <u>country</u>. _____

B. Write sentences using exact, vivid synonyms of the words in parentheses.

10. **(small)** _____

11. **(house)** _____

12. **(walk)** _____

Proofreading a Personal Narrative

PROOFREADING HINT

To be a good proofreader, look for one type of error at a time. For example, proofread once for capitalization errors, once for punctuation errors, and once for spelling errors.

Proofread the beginning of the personal narrative, paying special attention to spelling. Use the Proofreading Marks to correct at least seven errors.

PROOFREADING MARKS

◯	spell correctly
⊙	add period
?	add question mark
=	capitalize
℘	take out
∧	add
/	make lowercase
∿	switch
∧	add comma
∨ ∨	add quotation marks
¶	indent paragraph

See the chart on p. 4 to learn how to use these marks.

Last weekend I traveled more than a hunderd years back in time. No, I didn't find a time machine–I went to the Dickens Fair in San Francisco. The fare was held on Pier 45 at the famuos Fisherman's Wharf. The whole wharf was crowded with people, and everyone seemed to be having a grate time!

The people who worked at the Dickens Fair were all dressed the way people dressed in Engaland when Charles

Dickens was alive. The women wore long dresses, and most of the men had fancy hats. These people all spoke with English accents and used special phrases. My parents especially liked being greeted by people who said, "Hello, fair lady" and "Good day, kind sir."

there were some special booths at the dickens Fair. My older sister spent ours looking at the jewlry. Finally, she chose a pare of earrings. I had fun looking at all the booths, but I didn't by anything.

Make a Cause and Effect Chain

Write a series of causes and effects that tells a story. Write each sentence on a strip below.

Write about the Weather

Write an account of a recent weather event. Include details that give causes and effects. Include your feelings about what happened.

_____

_____

_____

_____

_____

_____

_____

_____

_____

_____

_____

_____

_____

_____

Write a Garden Journal

Imagine that you have a garden. Illustrate it in the garden plot provided. Plan and write a journal entry about a day of working with your plants and flowers. Revise and proofread your journal entry.

_____

_____

_____

_____

_____

_____

_____

_____

_____

_____

_____

_____

_____

_____

_____

_____

_____

Write from a Special Point of View

Pretend that you are a fork, a knife, a plate, a glass, or something else that is used at a table. With a friend, discuss how a meal would appear from your point of view. Together, write the story of a meal from that angle.

_____

_____

_____

_____

_____

_____

_____

_____

_____

_____

_____

_____

_____

A Practice Personal Paper

THE MYSTERIOUS ATLANTIC OCEAN FISH

I'm Benny, and here's my story. There's this kid, Sammy, who lives in the apartment across the hall. We don't have much to do with each other for one good reason. He's seven going on eight, and I'm ten going on eleven. He can do everything I like to do, but he's such a little kid. So I don't ask him to play ball with my friends, which is what I like to do most, because they wouldn't want a little kid on the team. Now you understand why we never get together.

One day last summer, my dad was talking to Sammy's dad. The next thing you know we're taking Sammy to the beach. "But my friends are coming over, Dad. We're going to play ball," I say. Then he says that I play ball every day and wouldn't I like to try something new for a change? I'm thinking no, but I don't say it. And before you know it, I'm on my way to the beach.

Sammy rolls his wheelchair into the crowded subway. My dad and I squeeze in, too. It seems like everyone in the city is going to the beach today. Wouldn't you know it? Well, we finally get off the train at Coney Island and go down to the beach with about one million other people. It takes forever before we find a place where we can put down our towels.

We've only been on our towels about 30 seconds before Sammy starts to smile. Pretty soon, he's laughing and having a great time. He finds a tide pool. It's a little pool of water the tide left when it went out. Anyhow, Sammy sees a small fish. After he watches it swim around a little, he scoops it up and plops it into his bucket. That's fine, except when it's time to leave, he wants to take the fish home. I tell him that's a terrible idea. How's an Atlantic Ocean fish going to live in a New York City apartment?

"We'll buy one of those big glass bowls," Sammy says.

"Wait," I say. "You don't get it. This is an Atlantic Ocean fish. It can only live in Atlantic Ocean water."

"So bring some Atlantic Ocean home with us," Sammy says.

Would you believe a smart guy like me actually lets a seven-going-on-eight kid talk him into filling two big buckets with water and dragging those buckets home on the subway? It's embarrassing.

So we buy a bowl and we fill it with Atlantic Ocean water. For about a week, the fish is swimming around pretty well. But as time passes, the fish isn't looking too terrific. Sammy says, "Benny, do something, do something," as if I'm a fish doctor or something. Hey, I can hardly keep my breakfast down when I see the guy at the fish store cleaning a fish. But Sammy won't leave me alone. He just keeps checking out his fish and calling me up with health reports about every 30 seconds.

Finally, he wears me down and I go have a look. You don't have to be a rocket scientist to figure out the problem is the water. At least half the Atlantic Ocean water I carried back in those buckets has evaporated.

Now we've got a real problem because there is no way I'm going back to the beach for more water. Besides, by the time I get out there and back, that fish will be in fish heaven. "Which is not a bad place," I tell Sammy, but that makes him cry.

Obviously, I need to take extreme measures. So I do the only thing I can do in an emergency like this. I fill a pitcher with New York City tap water and I dump the water into the bowl. I slush the tap water around so it mixes with the Atlantic Ocean water. Then I send out lots of good thoughts.

Sammy and I stare at the fish. By now, that fish is too sick to do anything except stare back. And that's the way we are for about a minute. We stare at the fish, and the fish stares back, and we get sadder and sadder, and the fish gets weaker and weaker.

I start making funeral plans. Then an amazing thing happens. Suddenly, the fish is swimming around the tank like it just got some really good news. It swims up, it swims down. It swims this way and that way. It practically does everything except somersault. I have to tell you. It was one amazing sight.

Now do you know why this story is called "The Mysterious Atlantic Ocean Fish"? Well, here's the mystery.

All winter I keep adding New York City water to the bowl. So after a while, with natural evaporation and all, it's clear there's no Atlantic Ocean water left. That saltwater fish is living and swimming in freshwater just as if it had been born in a sink. Is that amazing or what?

The other thing that's amazing is that Sammy and I got, well, you know, real close. Now we trade books, and we play video games. We do lots of stuff together. We even play ball with my other friends. As a matter of fact, Sammy decided that the next time we go to the beach, we'll take the whole team with us. I'm not sure that's a good idea. Can you imagine what he'll want us to help him bring back this time?

Respond to the Practice Paper

Write your answers to the following questions or directions.

1. Why did Benny write this story?

_____

_____

2. How did Benny feel in the beginning of the story? How do you know?

_____

_____

3. How did Benny feel at the end of the story? How do you know?

_____

_____

4. Write a paragraph to summarize the story. Use these questions to help
   you write your summary:

   - Who is the story about?
   - What are the main ideas in the story?
   - How does the story end?

_____

_____

_____

_____

_____

_____

_____

_____

Analyze the Practice Paper

Read "The Mysterious Atlantic Ocean Fish" again. As you read, think about how the writer wrote the story. Write your answers to the following questions.

1. How do you know that this is a personal narrative?

   _____

   _____

   _____

2. What is Benny's problem?

   _____

   _____

   _____

3. How does Benny solve his problem?

   _____

   _____

   _____

4. How does Benny keep your interest in the story?

   _____

   _____

   _____

5. How are the first paragraph and the last paragraph alike?

   _____

   _____

   _____

Writing Assignment

As people grow and change, they may have many best friends. Think about the best friend in your life now. Write a personal narrative that tells about your best friend. Use examples and details to show why this person is your best friend. Use this writing plan to help you write a first draft on the next page.

Name your friend:

▼

Tell how you and your friend became friends.

▼

Give examples to show why this person is your <u>best</u> friend.

First Draft

TIPS FOR WRITING A PERSONAL NARRATIVE:

- Write from your point of view. Use the words *I, me,* and *my* to show your readers that this is your story.

- Think about what you want to tell your reader.

- Organize your ideas into a beginning, middle, and end.

- Write an interesting introduction that "grabs" your readers.

- Write an ending for your story. Write it from your point of view.

Use your writing plan as a guide for writing your first draft of a personal narrative. Include a catchy title.

_____

_____

_____

_____

_____

_____

_____

_____

_____

(Continue on your own paper.)

Revise the Draft

Use the chart below to help you revise your draft. Check YES or NO to answer each question in the chart. If you answer NO, make notes to remind yourself how you can revise, or change, your writing to improve it.

Question	YES ✔	NO ✔	If the answer is NO, what will you do to improve your writing?
Does your story describe your best friend?			
Do you introduce your friend in the first paragraph?			
Do you describe events in the order they happened?			
Do you give examples to show why this person is your best friend?			
Do you include important details?			
Do you tell your story from your point of view? That is, do you use words such as *I, my*, and *me* to tell your story?			
Does your conclusion summarize your story in a new way?			
Have you corrected mistakes in spelling, grammar, and punctuation?			

Use the notes in your chart and your writing plan to revise your draft.

Writing Report Card

Read your revised draft again or ask someone else to read it. Have the person who reads your paper complete the following Report Card. Revise your paper until you have no less than a Very Good Score for each item.

Title of paper: _____

Purpose of paper: _*This is a personal narrative. It tells about*_

*my best friend.*

Person who scores the paper: _____

Score	Writing Goals
	Does the story have a strong beginning, or introduction?
	Are the story's main ideas organized into paragraphs?
	Are there details to support each main idea?
	Are the paragraphs organized in a way that makes sense?
	Are there different kinds of sentences that help make the story interesting?
	Is there a strong ending, or conclusion?
	Does the writer make it clear why the friend in this narrative is the writer's best friend?
	Are the story's grammar, spelling, and punctuation correct?

☺ Excellent Score   ☆ Very Good Score   + Good Score
✔ Acceptable Score   – Needs Improvement

UNIT 2: How-to Writing

HOW MUCH DO YOU KNOW?

These sentences from a how-to paragraph are out of order. Rewrite them in order in a paragraph, adding words and phrases from the box to make the order clear. Then answer the questions that follow.

Tie a knot in the balloon.
Stretch the balloon several times.
Hang it from the ribbon.
Pick out your favorite color of balloon.
Blow it up slowly.
Tie a ribbon around the knot.

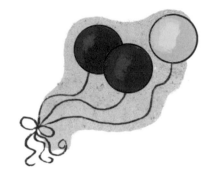

first	then	last
second	after that	the last thing
next	finally	the next thing you do
third	at the end	before you begin
at last	in the first place	

_____

_____

_____

_____

_____

1. What does this paragraph tell you how to do?

_____

2. What is the first thing you must do?

_____

Analyzing a How-to Paragraph

A HOW-TO PARAGRAPH

- gives instructions for making or doing something
- has a topic sentence, a list of materials, and step-by-step instructions with time-order words

Read the how-to paragraph. Answer the questions that follow.

Popping Popcorn in a Microwave Oven

Before you begin, make sure that you have popcorn that is especially packaged for microwave popping. Of course, you will need a microwave oven. Remove the plastic overwrap from the bag and place it in the center of the microwave. Be very careful not to puncture or open the special bag the popcorn is in. You should set the microwave for full, or 100 percent, power. Then set the timer for five minutes and push the button to start. Stop the microwave when popping time slows to two or three seconds between pops. Remove the hot bag from the oven. You should shake the bag before opening it to increase flavor and to distribute the salt.

1. How many items are listed as materials, and what are they?

   _____

2. What is the first thing you must do to make your microwave popcorn?

   _____

3. What is the next thing you do?

   _____

4. What happens next?

   _____

5. What do you do last?

   _____

Visualizing Steps in a Process

In a how-to paragraph, good writers picture the steps of an activity before writing directions for it.

These sentences from a how-to paragraph are out of order. Rewrite them in order in a paragraph, adding words and phrases from the box to make the order clear.

Get a bucket.

Dry the car.

To wash your family car, there are six steps you should follow.

Fill the bucket with soapy water.

Hose down the car to get it wet.

Shine the windows and any chrome trim.

Wash the car, using the soapy water and a soft cloth or sponge.

first
last
next
then
after that
finally
third
second
the last thing
the next thing you do
at the end
at last
before you begin
in the first place

_____

_____

_____

_____

_____

Writing for an Audience and a Purpose

GOOD WRITERS

- keep the intended audience in mind
- remember their purpose as they write

Read each version of a how-to paragraph below. Answer the questions that follow.

A. You will need an onion, a sharp knife, and a cutting board. First, peel the onion. Then, slice it in half lengthwise. Then, lay half of the onion cut-side down on the cutting board. Next, cut many lengthwise slices in it, being careful not to cut all the way through to the cutting board. Turn the onion around and cut crosswise slices in the opposite direction of the slices you just made. As you do this, the onion will break into small pieces.

B. You will need an onion, a sharp knife, and a cutting board. First, peel the onion and slice it in half. Next, cut lengthwise slices, and then cut crosswise slices in it. As you do this, the onion will break into small pieces.

1. Which version do you think is for a younger audience? Why?

   _____

2. Which version do you think is for an older audience? Why?

   _____

3. If Version A were for even younger readers, what information might be added?

   _____

Correcting Run-on Sentences

- Good writers avoid run-on sentences.
- Run-on sentences may be rewritten as simple sentences or as compound sentences.

Read each run-on sentence. Fix it in two ways. First write two simple sentences. Then write one compound sentence.

1. You'll need 101 index cards you'll need a colored marker.

   a. _____

   b. _____

2. Print the name of a state or a state capital on each index card print the rules on the last index card.

   a. _____

   b. _____

3. Put the marker away put all the cards in an envelope.

   a. _____

   b. _____

4. This game is for small groups up to three students may play.

   a. _____

   b. _____

5. Players mix up the cards they lay the cards face down.

   a. _____

   b. _____

Proofreading a How-to Paragraph

Proofread the how-to paragraphs, paying special attention to punctuation marks at the end of sentences. Use the Proofreading Marks to correct at least seven errors.

PROOFREADING MARKS	
⬭	spell correctly
⊙	add period
?	add question mark
≡	capitalize
୬	take out
∧	add
/	make lowercase
∿	switch
⋏	add comma
⌄ ⌄	add quotation marks
¶	indent paragraph

Do you have a little brother or sister Do

you sometimes help take care of little

children? If so, you might want to make a

set of special building blocks. These blocks

are large and light enough for even a two-

year-old to handle easaly. They are sturdy

and colorful, and they can be lots of fun

To make a set of blocks, you need as many half-gallon milk cartons you can collect. you also need sheets of colorful paper and some glue.

For each block, use two of your milk cartons Cut the tops off both cartons Then wash them thoroughly and let them dry Be sure your cartons are completely clean.

When both cartons are dry, push the open end of one cartoon into the other carton Press the two cartons together as far as possible. You should end up with a block that is the size of a single carton, with both ends closed and with extra-strong sides. Then cover each block, using glue and the paper you have chosen

Write about a Hobby

With a friend or two, make a list of hobbies you all enjoy. Choose one hobby you are familiar with. Plan and write a how-to paragraph about that hobby.

1. _____   2. _____

3. _____   4. _____

5. _____   6. _____

_____

_____

_____

_____

_____

_____

_____

_____

_____

_____

_____

_____

_____

Write about a Terrarium

With a friend or two, plan a terrarium. If necessary, do some library research to find out how to set it up. Write a how-to paragraph, and be sure to include each step needed to make the terrarium.

Write Pointers for Babysitters

With a friend or two, discuss what would be needed in a how-to manual for babysitters. Choose one area from your discussion and write about it. Illustrate your directions. Revise and proofread your work.

Write about Recycling

Think of ways you might recycle the items on the list into a how-to project. Write your ideas next to each item. Choose one idea and write a how-to paragraph about changing trash into a recycled treasure.

corks and bottle caps

_____

_____

worn-out sock

_____

_____

scraps of wrapping paper

_____

_____

_____

_____

_____

_____

_____

A Practice How-to Paper

HOW TO DECORATE A T-SHIRT

Decorating a T-shirt is easy to do, and you'll be proud to wear it. However, before you begin to work, you have some decisions to make.

First, where are you going to wear your T-shirt? Do you want to wear it to school? Do you want to make a T-shirt for a special occasion like a party? Do you want to make one to wear on a holiday like Valentine's Day?

Second, what do you want to put on your T-shirt? This question may be hard to answer because you have so many choices. All kinds of things go on T-shirts: names, sayings, cars, airplanes, trees, birds, people, rainbows. In fact, someone has probably drawn or printed almost anything you can think of on a T-shirt.

If you can't decide what to put on your T-shirt, think about your favorite foods. A big strawberry ice cream cone or a hot dog covered with chili and cheese would look great on a T-shirt.

If you don't want to wear your food, you might prefer to think about other favorite things, such as animals or flowers. You might draw a scene from your favorite book.

Maybe you don't want to draw anything at all. Perhaps you would prefer to make unusual designs. No matter what choice you make, a T-shirt can become a great painting.

The last thing you will need to think about is the colors you want to use. It's probably not a good idea to use too many colors. Otherwise, people will have to wear sunglasses to look at you.

By the time you have made your decisions, you are ready to

paint. Let's start with the materials you'll need.

Materials:

  1 white T-shirt

  8 in. x 8 in. piece of drawing paper

  pen or pencil

  2 safety pins

  transfer paper (Note: Transfer paper comes in a roll like waxed paper, so you can share a roll with your friends.)

  3 or 4 felt-tipped pens in different colors (Note: Felt-tipped pens come with different-sized tips. Use one with a thin tip to make outlines. Use pens with wider tips to fill in large spaces.)

Below are the steps you will follow.

1. Use a pen or pencil to draw your picture, design, or letters on the piece of drawing paper. Your drawing should be an outline. Do not fill it in. If you are printing letters, make sure they are in a straight line.

2. Now place your T-shirt on a hard surface. Make sure the front is smooth. Then lay a piece of transfer paper where you want your drawing to go. Make sure the piece of transfer paper is as big or bigger than the drawing paper.

3. Place your drawing over the transfer paper. Put one safety pin through the top of the drawing paper, the transfer paper, and the T-shirt. Put a second safety pin through the bottom of the drawing paper, the transfer paper, and the T-shirt. The pins will keep the two papers from moving.

4. Use the thin-tipped pen to go over the outline of your drawing or letters. Press firmly.

5. Remove the safety pins and drawing paper. You will see the outline of your drawing on the T-shirt. If the drawing isn't dark enough, trace over it again.

6. Use the colored felt-tipped pens to add color and details. The last step is the most fun. Enjoy wearing your new T-shirt!

Respond to the Practice Paper

Write your answers to the following questions or directions.

1. What does this how-to paper teach you to do?

   _____

2. What materials do you need?

   _____

   _____

   _____

3. What is the first decision you must make?

   _____

   _____

4. What is the second decision you must make?

   _____

   _____

5. What is the third decision you must make?

   _____

   _____

6. Write a paragraph to describe a T-shirt you would like to make. On a separate piece of paper, draw a picture to go with your paragraph.

   _____

   _____

   _____

   _____

   _____

Analyze the Practice Paper

Read "How to Decorate a T-Shirt" again. As you read, think about why the writer wrote this paper. What did the writer do to help explain how to decorate a T-shirt? Write your answers to the following questions or directions.

1. Why is this a good example of a how-to paper?

   _____

   _____

2. Why does the writer use words like *now*, *first*, and *second*?

   _____

   _____

3. Why does the writer list the materials you need to decorate a T-shirt?

   _____

   _____

4. Why does the writer list the steps you must follow to decorate a T-shirt?

   _____

   _____

5. Draw pictures to show the steps in decorating a T-shirt. Label each step.

Writing Assignment

Think about something you want to tell others how to do. Use this writing plan to help you write a first draft on the next page.

Tell what you want to tell others how to do.

List the materials you will need.

Write the steps someone should follow in order. Number the steps.

Write some sequence words that help the reader know what to do.

First Draft

TIPS FOR WRITING A HOW-TO PAPER:

- Choose one thing to teach someone.
- Focus on a plan.
    1. Think of all the materials someone will need.
    2. Think of all the steps someone will follow.
- Use sequence words in your directions.

Use your writing plan as a guide for writing your first draft of a how-to paper. Include a catchy title.

_____

_____

_____

_____

_____

_____

_____

_____

_____

(Continue on your own paper.)

Revise the Draft

Use the chart below to help you revise your draft. Check YES or NO to answer each question in the chart. If you answer NO, make notes to remind yourself how you can revise, or change, your writing to improve it.

Question	YES ✔	NO ✔	If the answer is NO, what will you do to improve your writing?
Does your paper teach how to do something?			
Do you use the first paragraph to introduce the project?			
Do you include the materials someone needs for this project?			
Do you describe all of the steps someone needs to follow?			
Do you write the steps in the order they should happen?			
Is each step written clearly to make it easy to follow?			
Do you use sequence words to make the directions easy to follow?			
Have you corrected mistakes in spelling, grammar, and punctuation?			

Use the notes in your chart and your writing plan to revise your draft.

Writing Report Card

Read your revised draft again or ask someone else to read it. Have the person who reads your paper complete the following Report Card. Revise your paper until you have no less than a Very Good Score for each item.

Title of paper: _____

Purpose of paper: _____*This paper explains how to do something.*_____

Person who scores the paper: _____

Score	Writing Goals
	Does the paper teach how to do something specific?
	Does the first paragraph explain what the paper will be about?
	Does the writer include the materials needed to do this task or project?
	Are the steps in order?
	Are there sequence words and/or numbers that make the directions easy to follow?
	Are there enough details for the reader to follow each step independently?
	Are the paper's grammar, spelling, and punctuation correct?

☺ Excellent Score ☆ Very Good Score + Good Score
✔ Acceptable Score – Needs Improvement

UNIT 3: Story

HOW MUCH DO YOU KNOW?

Read the story. Answer the questions that follow.

Paul Bunyan's helper, Juan, stared up at him and shook his head. "How will we ever get all this hot food to the tables?" Juan asked. "The dining hall is so big that the food gets cold before we can serve it."

"Why, that's easy," answered Paul. "We'll just put roller skates on the ponies. Then the ponies can skate in quickly and deliver the food before it gets cold."

"What a great idea!" cried Juan.

The next night, however, Paul and Juan discovered that Paul's idea wasn't great after all. The ponies weren't good roller skaters. They spilled most of the food, and then they stopped to eat the spilled food.

"What a mess!" exclaimed Paul.

"What will we do?" asked Juan.

"Well," said Paul, "first we'll have to clean up the dining hall. Then, I think we should build tracks between the rows of tables. We can use freight trains to deliver the food."

1. Who are the characters in the story?

   _____

2. What happens in the beginning?

   _____

   _____

3. What information does the writer give about Juan?

   a. _____

   _____

   b. _____

   _____

Analyzing a Humorous Story

> ## A HUMOROUS STORY
> - has a beginning, a middle, and an ending
> - achieves humor through language as well as through the characters and the plot

Read the story. Answer the questions that follow.

Once there was a man who thought his wife never did anything right. In fact, he didn't even think she could sneeze correctly. He criticized everything she did. One day the wife got so tired of listening to him that she suggested they trade jobs. The husband quickly agreed, saying it was the only good idea she had ever had.

The next morning the wife went out to the field to do the mowing. She worked very hard outside all morning, while the husband stayed at home to take care of the baby. By noon, the wife was hungry and was listening for the lunch bell.

Meanwhile, the husband was trying his best to bathe the baby. The water in the baby's bathtub ended up on the floor, and the husband used all the towels in the house to soak it up. He had no towels left to dry the baby, so he used diapers. He finally used the last diaper to put on the baby, but he couldn't get it to stay on. The last diaper ended up on the baby's head.

1. Who are the characters in the story?

   _____

2. What is the setting?

   _____

3. What is the general plot?

_____

4. What happens in the beginning?

_____

5. What happens in the end?

_____

_____

Using Details and Dialogue to Create Good Characters

GOOD WRITERS

- tell what the character says
- tell what other characters say about the character
- provide details of action

Read the story. How does the writer give information about Sal? Write each example below.

Aunt Susie looked all around for her nephew Sal. "Where has that boy gone?" she wondered. "He's always into some mischief, but I know he's a good boy deep down." Just then, she heard a sound from the other room. Sal ran out, wearing his bathing suit.

"Now, Sal," said Aunt Susie, "slow down. Where are you going in such a hurry? You know you have some chores to do. This Saturday will be different from last Saturday. You'll finish your work before you play."

"Oh, Aunt Susie," said Sal, looking at the floor. "You know I'll be sure to do it later. The sun is nice and hot now. This is the best time of day for a swim. Besides, all my friends are already at the lake."

After his swim, Sal fell asleep. When he woke up, he had forgotten his promise.

1. What the character says:

    a. _____

    b. _____

2. Details of action:

    a. _____

    b. _____

3. What other characters say about the character:

    a. _____

    b. _____

Expanding Sentences

Expand each sentence by adding at least one prepositional phrase. Begin your phrases with prepositions such as *above, after, before, between, during, for, from, in, on, of, over, through, under, up,* and *without.*

1. Gabrielle had a bad toothache.

   _____

2. Her mother drove her.

   _____

3. Gabrielle did not have to wait.

   _____

4. The dentist's assistant had her sit.

   _____

5. The assistant took an X-ray.

   _____

6. The dentist looked at the X-ray.

   _____

Proofreading a Tall Tale

PROOFREADING HINT

To be a good proofreader, look for one type of error at a time. For example, proofread once for capitalization errors, once for punctuation errors, and once for spelling errors.

Proofread the beginning of the tall tale, paying special attention to paragraph indents. Use the Proofreading Marks to correct at least seven errors.

PROOFREADING MARKS	
⬭	spell correctly
⊙	add period
?	add question mark
⹀	capitalize
℘	take out
∧	add
/	make lowercase
∿	switch
⋏	add comma
⌄ ⌄	add quotation marks
¶	indent paragraph

One of Paul Bunyan's helpers stared up at Paul and shook his head. "How will we ever get all this hot food two the tables?" he asked. The dining hall is so big that the food gets cold before we can serve it"

"Why, that's easy," answered Paul

"We'll just put roller skates on the ponies. Then the ponies can skate in quickly and deliver the food before it gets cold."

"What a great idea!" cried Paul Bunyan's helpers.

The next night, however, Paul and his helpers discovered that his idea

wasn't great after all. The ponies weren't good roller-skaters. They spilled

most of the food, and then they stopped to eat the spilled food.

"What a mess!" exclaimed Paul.

"What will we do?" asked his helpers.

Well, said Paul, "first, we'll have to clean up the dining hall. Then, I

think we should build tracks between the rose of tables. We can use freight

trains to deliver the food."

Write about Flying

Imagine that you can fly like a bird. With a friend or two, plan and write a humorous story about your imaginary flight. Include details and dialogue in your story.

(Continue on your own paper.)

Write an Amazing Explanation

Many tall tales explain how something in nature was created or formed. One amazing explanation shown below is from a Paul Bunyan tale. Choose one of the natural events and write an amazing explanation for it.

Natural Event	Amazing Explanation
an earthquake	Each time Paul Bunyan's cook dropped one of his biscuits, an earthquake occurred.
a volcanic eruption	_____ _____ _____
a hurricane	_____ _____ _____
Niagara Falls	_____ _____ _____

Write about People

With a friend, complete each of the following sentences. Use exaggeration to describe what each character does. The first one is done as an example. Then, decide which sentence you like best and develop it into a tall tale.

I know a <u>sailor</u> from <u>Monterey</u> who is so big that <u>he can wade across Monterey Bay</u>.

I know _____ from _____

who is so strong that _____.

I know _____ from _____

who is so tall that _____.

A TALL TALE

_____

_____

_____

_____

_____

_____

_____

_____

_____

_____

A Practice Fantasy Story

SEND THE CLONE

Tanisha stood with her hands on her hips. "How can I help you, Jemma, if you won't sit still?" Jemma sat on the edge of her bed. Her left leg stuck straight out. The lower half was wrapped in a thin sheet of metal. Tanisha tried to attach the top half.

"Sorry, Tanisha, I just hate wearing this thing. It makes my leg so stiff I can't move," answered Jemma.

"I think that's the point," Tanisha said as she stopped to look at Jemma. She shook her head. "It could have been a lot worse, you know. How many times has Coach warned you about playing in the anti-gravity chamber when she's not there?"

"Yeah, yeah, Tanisha. Gosh, you're as bad as my parents. I've already listened to all of their warnings. I think they're glad to see me wearing this. It means there's no chance I'll go in the chamber for a while."

"It also means you won't be able to practice for the physical fitness test," said Tanisha. "And you know what that means, don't you?" Tanisha stopped fastening the cast to look at Jemma again. Every year the fifth-grade class took a trip together. This year they were going to Mars.

"I know, I know. You have to be healthy to go. That means no broken bones. If I don't get out of this cast, I can't get in shape for the trip. And if I don't get in shape enough to pass the fitness test, then I don't get to go on the class trip. I thought of that, too. We practice the orbital launch test this week. How will I ever pass that if I don't practice first?" Jemma looked at Tanisha as though she had an answer. Actually, she did have an answer, but it wasn't the one Jemma wanted.

"You should have thought about that sooner. Now the only thing you can do is send your clone. Let her practice. Then you can download at night."

Jemma looked disappointed. "Tanisha, we both know what happens in a reverse download test. Do you remember what happened when I had to go to the dentist and sent my clone to take my French test?"

Tanisha laughed and slapped her hand on Jemma's cast. Jemma jumped. "That was a scream," Tanisha said, still laughing. "Who knew that French verbs could do that to electrical wiring? Madame Dejas had to hose her down to put out the fire. How many days did you stay after school that time?"

"Thanks for the reminder. Now get serious, Tanisha. What am I going to do?"

"I mean it," Tanisha said softly as she wiped the tears from her laughing eyes. "Send your clone. It's the only thing you can do. Then download after class each day. It's risky, but what choice do you have? If she crashes, you can re-program her."

"Right, but then I lose everything. It takes days of downloading to restore my clone's memory. I'm already twelve, you know. I've stored twelve years of information in my brain."

"Well, it's up to you. But the way I see it, you don't have a choice. It's either send the clone or miss the class trip," said Tanisha.

"Tanisha, if I miss the trip, you wouldn't go without me, would you?" Jemma asked. Jemma's eyes were wide. Surely, her friend wouldn't go without her. Jemma didn't have to wait long for an answer.

"Are you kidding? Do you know how long I've waited for fifth grade just so I could go on this trip?"

Once again, Jemma looked disappointed. It looked as if she'd end up spending spring break at home with her clone. Tanisha saw the sad look on Jemma's face. "Don't give up, Jemma. Let's try my plan. If it doesn't work, well, I'll send you a postcard."

Jemma looked disgusted. "Some friend you are. Help me get her ready, would you?"

Tanisha turned on the clone to let her warm up. "She seems to be working fine this morning," she said. "The lights are on. The battery check is fine. This could work, you know," she said to Jemma. "Hey, I have another idea."

"If it's better than your first idea, tell me," said Jemma. For a moment, Jemma was hopeful.

"Well, if your clone passes the fitness test, she can go on the trip instead. Then you can download the entire experience." Tanisha started laughing again.

"Very funny," Jemma said as she tried not to laugh. She stood awkwardly and smoothed her school uniform. "Let's get going. My clone and I have to be at the launch pad when first period starts."

Respond to the Practice Paper

Write your answers to the following questions or directions.

1. A fantasy is a kind of imaginative story. It takes the reader into a world that isn't real. Explain why this story is an example of a fantasy.

   _____

   _____

2. What is the setting for this story?

   _____

   _____

3. What is the main character's problem in this story?

   _____

   _____

4. How is the main character's problem solved?

   _____

   _____

5. Write a paragraph to summarize the story. Use these questions to help you write your summary:
   • What is the story about?
   • What happens first? Second? Third?
   • How does the story end?

   _____

   _____

   _____

   _____

   _____

Analyze the Practice Paper

Read "Send the Clone" again. As you read, think about how the writer wrote the story. Answer the following questions or directions.

1. What did the writer do to make this story seem believable?

   _____

   _____

   _____

2. What did the writer do to make this story seem unbelievable?

   _____

   _____

   _____

3. Why do you think the writer uses mostly dialogue, or conversation, to tell this story?

   _____

   _____

   _____

4. What mood, or feeling, does the writer create in this story? Give an example to support your answer.

   _____

   _____

   _____

Writing Assignment

Writing stories lets us use our imaginations. Use your imagination to write a fantasy story. Think about the answers to the questions below. Use this writing plan to help you write a first draft on the next page.

Where will your story take place?

▼

What characters will you use?

▼

How will you make the story believable?

▼

How will you make the story unbelievable?

▼

What problem will the characters have? How will they solve it? List and number the steps in the story.

First Draft

Use your writing plan as a guide for writing your first draft of a fantasy. Include a catchy title.

_____

_____

_____

_____

_____

_____

_____

_____

_____

(Continue on your own paper.)

Revise the Draft

Use the chart below to help you revise your draft. Check YES or NO to answer each question in the chart. If you answer NO, make notes to remind yourself how you can revise, or change, your writing to improve it.

Question	YES ✔	NO ✔	If the answer is NO, what will you do to improve your writing?
Does your story happen in a world that isn't real?			
Is your story believable?			
Do you use an interesting plot to keep the reader's attention?			
Are your characters interesting?			
Do your characters have a problem?			
Do your characters solve their problem?			
Do you describe what happens in order?			
Is the story imaginative?			
Have you corrected mistakes in spelling, grammar, and punctuation?			

Use the notes in your chart and your writing plan to revise your draft.

Writing Report Card

Read your revised draft again or ask someone else to read it. Have the person who reads your paper complete the following Report Card. Revise your paper until you have no less than a Very Good Score for each item.

Title of paper: _____

Purpose of paper: ___*This story is a fantasy.*_____

Person who scores the paper: _____

Score	Writing Goals
	Does the story happen in a world that isn't real?
	Is the story believable?
	Does the story have an interesting setting?
	Are the characters interesting?
	Do the characters have a problem they must solve?
	Do the characters solve their problem?
	Do things happen in the story in order?
	Does the story keep your interest?
	Is the story imaginative?
	Are the story's grammar, spelling, and punctuation correct?

☺ Excellent Score   ☆ Very Good Score   + Good Score
✔ Acceptable Score   − Needs Improvement

UNIT 4: Comparative Writing

HOW MUCH DO YOU KNOW?

Read the paragraph of comparison and contrast. Answer the questions that follow.

    The first time LeAnn went to visit her friend Vanessa, she noticed how much Vanessa's furniture was like her own. The dresser in Vanessa's room was made of pine, just like LeAnn's dresser. Vanessa's aunt had chosen the dresser, just as LeAnn's aunt had chosen LeAnn's. LeAnn also noticed the desk in Vanessa's room. Vanessa said that it had been her grandfather's desk. LeAnn remembered that the desk in her own room had once belonged to her grandmother.

    As LeAnn looked at Vanessa's desk, she pictured her own desk in her mind. LeAnn's desk was a graceful old rolltop. Vanessa's desk, on the other hand, was dark and heavy with a huge flat surface. LeAnn realized that she would rather have a desk like Vanessa's. The flat top was much better for holding a computer screen and keyboard. As soon as LeAnn got a computer, she decided, she would put her grandmother's desk into her brother's room.

1. What is the topic sentence of the first paragraph?

   _____

   _____

2. List two ways in which the dressers are alike.

   _____

   _____

3. List one way in which the desks are different.

   _____

   _____

Analyzing Paragraphs of Comparison and Contrast

A paragraph of comparison
compares things (shows their similarities).

A paragraph of comparison
contrasts things (shows their differences).

Read the paragraph of comparison and contrast. Answer the questions that follow.

The Tasady tribe and the Ik tribe are two examples of people still living in the Stone Age. Neither tribe knew anything about the outside world until recently. The Tasady live in the mountain caves of the Philippine rain forests. The Ik live in the mountains of Uganda, and they build grass huts for shelter. There is plenty of food in the Philippine rain forests, so the Tasady are comfortable and fairly well off. The Ik, however, face a constant lack of food. Ik usually eat any food they find right away. The Tasady have a good chance of surviving; the Ik, on the other hand, face an uncertain future.

1. What two things are being compared?

   _____

2. What are three things that are alike in each?

   _____

   _____

3. What are three things that are different?

   _____

   _____

4. Does the last sentence of the paragraph compare or contrast the survival of the tribes?

   _____

Evaluating to Compare and Contrast

BEFORE COMPARING OR CONTRASTING TWO THINGS, GOOD WRITERS

- observe how they are alike and how they are different
- evaluate them in terms of some of their important qualities

Think about each pair of things. List two ways in which the things are alike and two ways in which they are different.

LIKENESSES	DIFFERENCES

1. a cloud and a kite

    a. _____   a. _____

    b. _____   b. _____

2. a book and a movie

    a. _____   a. _____

    b. _____   b. _____

3. rain and snow

    a. _____   a. _____

    b. _____   b. _____

4. morning and evening

    a. _____   a. _____

    b. _____   b. _____

5. basketball and baseball

    a. _____   a. _____

    b. _____   b. _____

6. broccoli and cauliflower

    a. _____   a. _____

    b. _____   b. _____

Using Formal and Informal Language

GOOD WRITERS CHANGE THEIR WRITING TO USE

- formal language to communicate in an official way
- informal language to communicate in a casual way

Read each sentence. Write *formal* or *informal* to describe the tone of each sentence.

1. At an early age Kit Carson learned how to work with leather. _____

2. "This notion of working in a leather shop is for the birds," young Kit said to himself. _____

3. "I'm getting out of here the first chance I get!" he vowed. _____

4. Kit Carson's real ambition was to be a mountain man. _____

5. He wanted to choose his own company and go where he pleased. _____

6. "I figure if we march west from here, we'll soon hit California," said one of the men. _____

7. The mountain men started their westward push. _____

8. Kit Carson was the youngest man in the group. _____

9. They could not carry much water with them. _____

10. "It's going to be a long dry spell," thought Kit. _____

11. They continued to look for signs of water. _____

Making Compound Sentences

Good writers show their audience the connection between ideas by joining two related sentences with a conjunction and a comma.

Use a comma and the word *and* to join each pair of sentences. Write the new sentence.

1. The Pygmies live in the forest in Africa. They hunt there.

   _____

   _____

2. Pygmy men are about four and a half feet tall. The women are even smaller.

   _____

   _____

3. They are the smallest people in the world. Their small size helps them to hide.

   _____

   _____

4. Children the same age call boys "brother." They call girls "sister."

   _____

   _____

5. Pygmies look at a broken branch. They can tell which animal has been there.

   _____

   _____

6. Pygmies know a lot about plants. They can tell which are good to eat.

   _____

   _____

Proofreading Paragraphs that Compare and Contrast

PROOFREADING MARKS	
⬭	spell correctly
⊙	add period
?	add question mark
≡	capitalize
℘	take out
∧	add
/	make lowercase
∼	switch
⋏	add comma
ᵛ ᵛ	add quotation marks
¶	indent paragraph

Proofread the paragraphs that compare and contrast, paying special attention to apostrophes in possessive nouns. Use the Proofreading Marks to correct at least seven errors.

The first time Lee went visit his friend Vladimir, he noticed how much Vlad's furniture was like his own. He saw that the desk in Vlads room was made of pine, just like Lees desk. Vlad's mom had chosen the desk, just as lee's mom had chosen Lee's. Lee also noticed the bed in Vlads room. Vlad explained that it had been his grandfathers bed. Lee

remembered that the bed in his own room had once belonged to his dad's

dad

As Lee looked at Vlads bed, he pictured his own bed in his mind. Lee's

bed was made of brass and steel. It had been made in England more then

100 years ago. Vlad's desk, on the other hand, was dark wood with a tall

hedboard It had been made in Russia about 60 years ago. Lee realized that

he would rather have a bed like Vlads. The headboard was good for

holding books.

Make Comparisons

Work with two friends. Discuss how each of you is similar to and different from the others. Together, write a paragraph comparing and contrasting your similarities and differences. Revise and proofread your work.

_____

_____

_____

_____

_____

_____

_____

_____

_____

_____

_____

_____

_____

_____

_____

_____

_____

Write a Diary Entry

Imagine that you must leave your country to go to another. Plan and write a diary entry comparing and contrasting your present country with the new country. Revise and proofread your work.

_____

_____

_____

_____

_____

_____

_____

_____

_____

_____

_____

_____

_____

_____

Compare Wildlife

Make a list of wildlife for each category below. Research two animals from one category. Write a paragraph of comparison and contrast using the information you learned.

LAND ANIMALS	BIRDS	INSECTS
_____	_____	_____
_____	_____	_____
_____	_____	_____
_____	_____	_____

_____

_____

_____

_____

_____

_____

_____

A Practice Compare-and-Contrast Paper

THE AMERICAN BLACK BEAR AND THE POLAR BEAR

The most famous bear in the world may be the teddy bear. Almost 100 years ago, President Theodore, or Teddy, Roosevelt was hunting bears in the Mississippi woods. The only bear he found was old, and the president wouldn't shoot it. A newspaper reporter drew a cartoon showing this event. Many people saw it. One of these people was Morris Michtom. He was a shopkeeper whose wife made stuffed bears. Morris got permission from the president to call the stuffed bears "teddy bears." A tradition was born.

The next best-known North American bear is the American black bear. But perhaps the most popular bear at zoos is the polar bear. Both bears are alike in some ways, and different, too. Let's look at them more closely.

American black bears live in most states and throughout Canada. They live in forests that have lots of undergrowth, or low-lying plants. Polar bears live along the northern coasts of Canada, Greenland, and Siberia. They are also on islands in the Arctic Ocean. Polar bears like plenty of ice.

An adult male black bear stands between 3 and 4 feet tall. It weighs between 135 and 350 pounds. An adult male polar bear stands 8 to 11 feet tall. That's probably higher than the ceiling in your classroom. Some male polar bears weigh more than 1,000 pounds. A polar bear is a real heavyweight.

You won't be surprised to learn that many black bears have black fur coats. However, they can be other colors, too. They can be chocolate brown, cinnamon, blond, and silver gray.

Polar bears have thick fur that looks white or yellow, but it isn't. Each hair is a clear, hollow tube. The tube lets the sun's rays reach the bear's skin. The sunlight and seal oil can make the fur look yellow.

Both black bears and polar bears have a good sense of smell. As many visitors to U.S. national parks can tell you, black bears are good at finding food. They can find food in any campsite, even when the food is hidden. They also learn to recognize the containers food comes in. That's why they open car doors, ice chests, and coolers.

Polar bears can smell food that is as far as 10 miles away. They can also sniff out seal dens that are covered by thick layers of snow and ice.

Black bears and polar bears use their sense of smell to find different things to eat. Black bears like berries, nuts, grass, and other plants. They may also eat small animals and fish. Sometimes they'll eat dead animals left by other animals, such as cougars. In the fall, black bears eat a lot. They may gain as many as 30 pounds each week. The extra pounds come from fat stored in their bodies. The bears use this fat for energy while they hibernate, or nap, through the winter.

Polar bears are meat-eaters. They feed mainly on small seals called ringed seals. They eat the seal's skin and fat, and leave the meat for other animals. Polar bears need to eat at least 1 pound of fat each day for energy. Sometimes polar bears eat walruses or the remains of dead animals, such as whales. Their sense of smell helps them find remains that are many miles away.

Male and female black bears hibernate in the winter. They spend 5 to 7 months napping. Only pregnant female polar bears hibernate. The other females and males are active all year, even during the winter.

Black bears are usually born in January or February. Twins are common, and the cubs are born blind and small. Each cub weighs less than 1 pound, but it grows fast. Female polar bears usually have twin cubs, too. They are often born in December or January. Polar bear cubs are also born blind and small. Each cub weighs about $1\frac{1}{2}$ pounds. Like black bear cubs, polar bear cubs grow fast.

Today there are far fewer black bears than there were when colonists came to America. Colonists in the East hunted the bears almost to extinction. That means the bears almost disappeared entirely. In the last 30 years, scientists have learned much more about black bears. The number of black bears is growing again, but the bears are still in danger.

Polar bears are also in danger of disappearing. According to scientists, there are about 28,000 polar bears in the world. To protect them, the United States works with Canada and other countries in the world.

American black bears and polar bears are alike in many ways. They are large, smart animals with sharp senses. They have small babies that grow fast. They are also wonderful models for the stuffed bears we love so much.

Respond to the Practice Paper

Summarize the paper by making a chart. Use the chart below to list ways American black bears and polar bears are alike and different.

**AN ALIKE AND DIFFERENT CHART FOR
AMERICAN BLACK BEARS AND POLAR BEARS**

How American Black Bears and Polar Bears Are Alike	How American Black Bears and Polar Bears Are Different

Analyze the Practice Paper

Read "The American Black Bear and the Polar Bear" again. As you read, think about how the writer achieved his or her purpose for writing. Write your answers to the following questions.

1. Why do you think the writer begins this paper by talking about teddy bears?

   _____

   _____

2. How did the writer relate teddy bears to the real bears described in this paper?

   _____

   _____

3. What main idea is discussed in the fifth and sixth paragraphs?

   _____

   _____

4. Read the ninth paragraph again. How does the writer let you know what this paragraph and the tenth paragraph will be about?

   _____

   _____

5. The writer uses the last paragraph to summarize the main ideas in the paper. What else does the writer do in the last paragraph?

   _____

   _____

   _____

   _____

Writing Assignment

Think about two animals you would like to write about. Write about how they are alike and how they are different. Use this writing plan to help you write a first draft on page 82.

Choose two animals you want to write about. Call them A and B.

A = _____   B = _____

Use reference materials or the Internet to learn more about A and B. Learn about these main ideas: 1. how the animals look, 2. where the animals live, and 3. what the animals eat. For each main idea, list what is true only about A in the A circle. List what is true only about B in the B circle. List what is true about both A and B where the two circles overlap. If you have more than three main ideas, draw and label more diagrams on a separate sheet of paper.

MAIN IDEA:
How the animals look

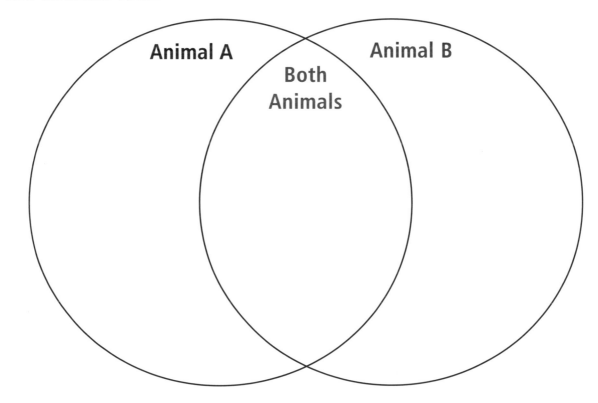

MAIN IDEA:
Where the animals live

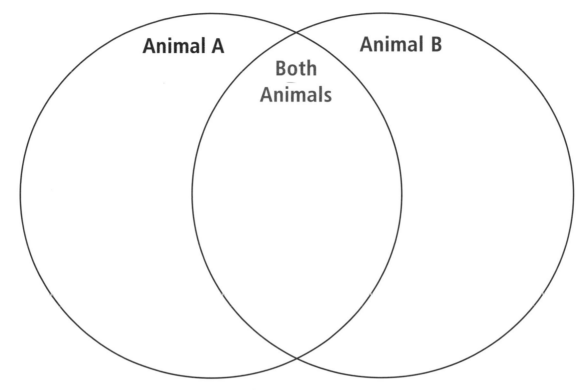

Animal A **Animal B**

Both Animals

MAIN IDEA:
What the animals eat

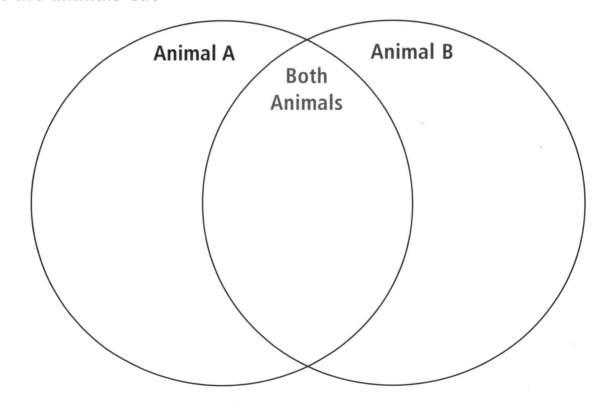

Animal A **Animal B**

Both Animals

First Draft

Use your writing plan as a guide for writing your first draft of a compare-and-contrast paper. Include a catchy title.

_____

_____

_____

_____

_____

_____

_____

_____

_____

_____

(Continue on your own paper.)

Revise the Draft

Use the chart below to help you revise your draft. Check YES or NO to answer each question in the chart. If you answer NO, make notes to remind yourself how you can revise, or change, your writing to improve it.

Question	YES ✔	NO ✔	If the answer is NO, what will you do to improve your writing?
Do you introduce the animals you will write about in your first paragraph?			
Does your paper tell how the two animals are alike?			
Does your paper tell how the two animals are different?			
Do you have more than one main idea?			
Do you organize the main ideas into paragraphs?			
Do you use details to support each main idea?			
Do you use the last paragraph to summarize the main ideas of your paper in a new way?			
Do you tie the first and last paragraphs together?			
Have you corrected mistakes in spelling, grammar, and punctuation?			

Use the notes in your chart and your writing plan to revise your draft.

Writing Report Card

Read your revised draft again or ask someone else to read it. Have the person who reads your paper complete the following Report Card. Revise your paper until you have no less than a Very Good Score for each item.

Title of paper: _____

Purpose of paper: _*This paper tells how two animals are*_ _____

*alike and different.* _____

Person who scores the paper: _____

Score	Writing Goals
	Does the first paragraph tell what the paper is about?
	Does the paper tell how two animals are alike?
	Does the paper tell how two animals are different?
	Is there more than one main idea?
	Are the main ideas organized into paragraphs?
	Are there enough details to support each main idea?
	Are the paragraphs in an order that makes sense?
	Does the last paragraph summarize what the paper is about?
	Are the paper's grammar, spelling, and punctuation correct?

☺ Excellent Score   ☆ Very Good Score   + Good Score
✔ Acceptable Score   − Needs Improvement

UNIT 5: Descriptive Writing

HOW MUCH DO YOU KNOW?

Read the paragraph. Answer the questions that follow.

A box turtle is a reptile that lives in woods and fields. The box turtle has a hinged lower shell. It can pull its legs, head, and tail inside its shell and get "boxed in." Box turtles eat earthworms, insects, berries, and green leafy vegetables. There are many kinds of turtles on land and in the water. Turtles belong to the same family as lizards, snakes, alligators, and crocodiles.

1. What is being described?

   _____

   _____

2. What are three details?

   a. _____

   _____

   b. _____

   _____

   c. _____

   _____

Read each sentence. On the line, write each underlined word and tell the sense or senses to which it most appeals as it is used in the sentence.

3. I picked up the smooth, hard turtle shell.

   _____

4. There was a rustle of leaves before a loud splash, so I knew the turtle had gone into the lake.

   _____

Analyzing a Descriptive Paragraph

A DESCRIPTIVE PARAGRAPH
- describes someone or something
- has a topic sentence that tells what is being described
- gives sensory details that offer specific information about the subject

Read each paragraph. Answer the questions that follow. You need not write the whole sentence when listing the details.

Thanksgiving has to be my favorite holiday. The delicious aromas of turkey roasting and pumpkin pies baking fill the house. The lovely autumn colors of orange, gold, red, and brown can be seen in the special flower arrangements for the table. The sound of children laughing as they play games outside mixes with the music being played inside. The sights, smells, and sounds are very important to me.

1. What is being described? _____

2. What is the topic sentence? _____

3. What are three details?

    a. _____

    b. _____

    c. _____

Did you ever walk into the kitchen of a good cook just before a special feast? "Here, sample this. What do you think?" the cook might say as you walk in. Then you are treated to a sweet taste of a dessert sauce, a tasty sample of rich gravy, or a yummy mouthful of fresh beets just steamed. Maybe you'll get to taste some fresh, warm bread. You might be full before dinner is even ready!

4. What is being described?

_____

5. What is the topic sentence?

_____

_____

Observing Details in Spatial Order

A. Read each description. Write *left to right, back to front,* **or** *top to bottom* **to tell how the writer organized the details.**

1. The judges watched as the runners warmed up for the race. Over on the left, Bobby Malone from Bingham Elementary was touching his toes. Next to him, Mario Gilbert from Stratford Grade School was stretching. On the right, Stuart Meyers from the Drayer School for the Hearing Impaired was bending and stretching.

   _____

2. Of the three runners, Stu Meyers had the best chance of winning. From the short-cropped hair on his head to his slim torso and long legs, he seemed to be in the best physical shape.

   _____

B. Write short descriptions of the item below. Use each of the methods for organizing details in space order.

3. YOUR CLASSROOM

   left to right: _____

   _____

4. back to front: _____

   _____

5. top to bottom: _____

   _____

Using Sensory Images

Good writers use sensory words that appeal to some or all of the five senses.

Read each sentence. On the line, write each underlined word and tell the sense or senses to which it most appeals as it is used in the sentence.

1. The young swimmer was wearing a <u>blue</u> <u>suit</u>.

   _____

2. She dove cleanly into the <u>cool</u> <u>water</u>.

   _____

3. The judges wrote the scores in <u>large</u> <u>black</u> letters.

   _____

4. The audience let out a <u>loud</u> cheer.

   _____

5. She had been practicing so long, her <u>hair</u> had the odor of <u>chlorine</u>.

   _____

6. One tile on her practice pool was <u>rough</u> and <u>jagged</u>.

   _____

7. The rough edge had cut her <u>foot</u>, and she had <u>yelled</u>, "Ouch!"

   _____

8. Her coach had put a <u>soft</u> <u>bandage</u> on it, and it was fine now.

   _____

9. The sweatshirt she put on was <u>warm</u> and <u>soft</u>.

   _____

10. After practice, she had had a <u>delicious</u> <u>sandwich</u>.

    _____

Combining Subjects and Predicates

GOOD WRITERS
- write concisely, avoiding unnecessary repetition
- combine subjects and predicates to make their writing smoother and more direct

Rewrite each of the following sentence pairs. Combine subjects and predicates to make sentences that are more concise.

1. Young Soren rolled in the grass under a tree. Young Soren watched the sailboats.

   _____

   _____

2. Some ships were going to Baltimore. Some ships were sailing out to sea.

   _____

   _____

3. Young Soren did not know what a geography book was. Young Soren did not know what an arithmetic book was.

   _____

   _____

4. He had never been to school. He had never learned how to read.

   _____

   _____

5. The hill was a good place to stand. The hill was a good place to watch the boats.

   _____

   _____

6. Soren visited his grandmother in the summer. Soren visited his uncle in the winter.

   _____

   _____

Proofreading a Descriptive Paragraph

Proofread the descriptive paragraphs, paying special attention to capital letters in proper nouns. Use the Proofreading Marks to correct at least seven errors.

PROOFREADING MARKS	
◯	spell correctly
⊙	add period
?	add question mark
≡	capitalize
℘	take out
∧	add
/	make lowercase
∿	switch
⋏	add comma
˅ ˅	add quotation marks
¶	indent paragraph

Aunt jane said she would have a surprise for us last saturday, but she refused to give us any hints. Just after breakfast, we heard a low humming sound in our driveway. It was followed by an unusual, squeaky car horn. A car! A car!" my Sister shouted. "Aunt Jane's surprise is a Car!"

We all rushed out to see Aunt Jane's new car, and what a surprise it was! Her "new" car was more than 50 years old. It was a beautiful 1938

whippet. Its bright green surface shimmered in the sunlight. Its long hood stretched forward elegantly, and its whitewall tires gleamed on our dusty driveway

"Oh, jane," said mom. "What a great car! May we get in?"

"Of course," laughed Aunt Jane, and she clicked the front door open for us. The inside of the car was dark and cool and filled with the soft smell of old lether.

"Let's go for a drive," suggested dad. "Who wants to ride out to Lake barton?"

Describe an Unusual Animal

Plan and write a description of an unusual animal. Draw a picture to go with your description. Revise and proofread your work.

Make a Sense Poster

Look at the boxes below labeled *smell*, *sight*, and *hearing*. Using old magazines, cut out one picture that appeals to each sense. Paste each picture in a section and write three sentences to describe the item as related to that sense.

SMELL

_____
_____
_____
_____
_____
_____

SIGHT

_____
_____
_____
_____
_____
_____

HEARING

_____
_____
_____
_____
_____

Describe the Same Scene in Different Ways

With a friend, draft a description of an athletic event from two different points of view: from the field or court and from the spectator stands. Compare the descriptions.

From the field or court

_____

_____

_____

_____

_____

_____

_____

From the spectator stands

_____

_____

_____

_____

_____

_____

_____

_____

Describe a Natural Event

Choose a common natural event, such as a sunset, a rainstorm, or the growth of a tree. Write a description of that natural event. Remember to use sensory details.

_____

_____

_____

_____

_____

_____

_____

_____

_____

_____

                                            _____

                                            _____

                                            _____

                                            _____

                                            _____

A Practice Descriptive Story

THE TRAVELING GONZALEZ FAMILY

The Gonzalez family loved to travel. Every year they sat down and decided where they wanted to go on their vacation. Usually, they agreed on one place. But this year everyone had a different idea.

"I want to go to California and see the Pacific Ocean," Miguel said.

"Who cares what you want?" said Angela. "You're only eight. I'm eleven and I get to decide. I want to see the White House."

"How about me?" said Mrs. Gonzalez. "I want to go to Arizona and see a rodeo."

"That sounds interesting," said Mr. Gonzalez, "but I would rather go to Yellowstone National Park. Old Faithful, the geyser, is there."

"We have a problem," everyone said. They all looked at each other. "What shall we do?" asked Miguel.

"I have an idea," said Mrs. Gonzalez. "I think I know how we can see all those places."

"Impossible," everyone said. But they agreed to give Mrs. Gonzalez a chance.

The next day they found themselves in front of a very large building. "Now hang onto each other and follow the person in front of you," said Mrs. Gonzalez. "And," she added, "keep your eyes closed until I say open."

The family walked and walked. Finally, Mrs. Gonzalez said, "Open your eyes." There in front of them was the beautiful Pacific Ocean. Its deep, blue-green water looked as smooth as silk. In the distance, two fishers stood in a small fishing boat. They were pulling in a net filled with slick, squirming fish. A flock of gulls soared above the boat. Their feathers reflected the setting sun, making them shine with red and gold light. They swooped and dived toward the boat, waiting for the fishers to throw unwanted fish back into the water.

"This is the most beautiful ocean in the world," Miguel said. Everyone agreed.

"Now close your eyes again," Mrs. Gonzalez said. "We're off to the rodeo."

When everyone opened their eyes, the first thing the family saw was a cowgirl. She and her horse were racing around huge, wooden barrels. The girl's hat sat over her eyes to shade them from the sun. One of her hands gripped the front of the saddle. The other hand waved high in the air. Her horse leaned from side to side. It moved quickly around the first of three barrels, raising a cloud of dirt and pebbles. Behind the horse and rider, the crowd was on its feet, cheering her on. "The rider who races around the three barrels the fastest wins," Mrs. Gonzalez explained.

"I never saw anything so exciting," said Angela. "This is fun!"

"When are we going to Yellowstone Park?" asked Mr. Gonzalez.

"That's our next stop," said Mrs. Gonzalez. "Close your eyes."

When Mrs. Gonzalez said open, everyone whispered, "Ooooh." There in front of them was Yellowstone Canyon. Great splashes of yellow, red, white, orange, and brown peeked through the green of the forest.

"Where's Old Faithful Geyser?" Angela asked.

"Over here," said Mr. Gonzalez. Mr. Gonzalez pointed to the

right. Everyone's eyes turned with his finger. There was Old Faithful Geyser sending a silvery shower of steaming water high into the air. "That spout is as high as a fifteen-story building," Mr. Gonzalez said.

"Speaking of big buildings," Angela said. "When are we going to Washington, D.C.?"

"Next stop, the capital," said Mrs. Gonzalez. Soon the family was in the middle of gardens, parks, and monuments. In the distance, the White House shimmered in the light. A huge flag flapped quietly in a gentle breeze. There were people everywhere. Angela could tell they were on vacation, too. They carried cameras and backpacks. Some had brought picnics and sat in the parks. Someone nearby munched a delicious-looking sandwich.

"I can't go any farther. I'm hungry," Miguel said.

"Well, we can take care of that," said Mr. Gonzalez.

Later that evening, when they were finishing supper, Mrs. Gonzalez said, "Do you know where I took you today?"

"I know," said Miguel.

"I know," said Mr. Gonzalez.

"Me, too," said Angela. "It was my first trip to an art museum. I'm going to take vacations more often. The museum is free on Sunday afternoon. I thought I'd go again this weekend. Who wants to go with me?" Everyone raised a hand.

Respond to the Practice Paper

Write your answers to the following questions or directions.

1. What does the writer describe in this story?

   _____

   _____

2. What was the problem Mrs. Gonzalez had to solve?

   _____

   _____

3. Where did each person in the family want to go?

   _____

   _____

4. How did Mrs. Gonzalez solve her family's problem?

   _____

   _____

5. Write a paragraph to summarize the story. Use these questions to help you write your summary.

   • What are the main ideas of this story?
   • What happens first? Second? Third?
   • How does the story end?

   _____

   _____

   _____

   _____

   _____

Analyze the Practice Paper

Read "The Traveling Gonzalez Family" again. As you read, think about how the writer achieved his or her purpose for writing. Write your answers to the following questions or directions.

1. What are some exciting action words the writer uses?

   _____

   _____

2. What are some descriptions the writer uses to help you imagine what the family is seeing?

   _____

   _____

3. In the tenth paragraph, the writer describes seagulls. The writer says, "Their feathers reflected the setting sun, making them shine with red and gold light." What is another way the writer could describe the gulls' feathers?

   _____

   _____

4. The writer has Mr. Gonzalez say that when Old Faithful spouts, it is as "high as a fifteen-story building." What is another way the writer could have described how high the geyser spouts?

   _____

   _____

5. This story has a surprise ending. What would another good surprise ending for this story be?

   _____

   _____

Writing Assignment

To describe something, a writer tells what he or she sees, hears, feels, tastes, and smells. The writer also compares things to other things, like a geyser to a silvery shower. Write about an experience that you would like to describe. Pay special attention to the words you choose. Use this writing plan to help you write a first draft on the next page.

What experience would you like to describe? Write it in the circle. Then write words and comparisons that describe the experience on the lines.

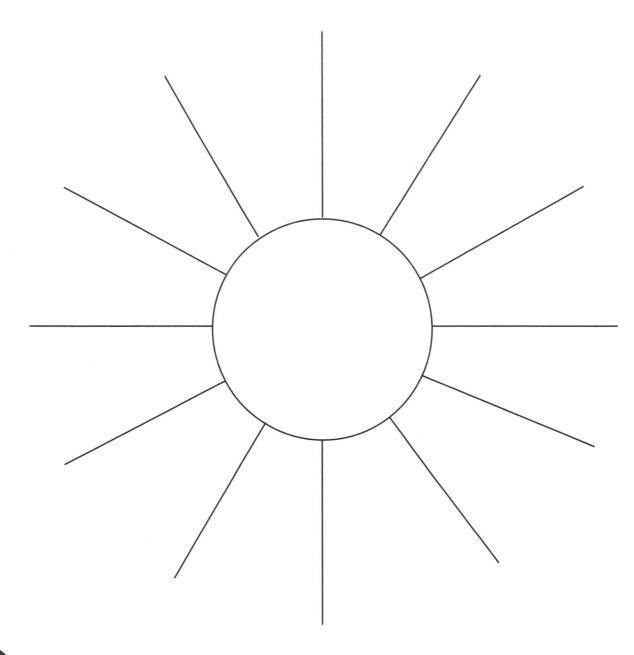

First Draft

TIPS FOR WRITING A DESCRIPTIVE STORY:

- Use your voice when you write. That means you should use your special way of expressing yourself.

- Help your reader see, smell, taste, feel, and hear what you are writing about.

- Use interesting words, similes, and metaphors to help describe your experience.

Use your writing plan as a guide as you write your first draft of a descriptive story. Include a catchy title.

_____

_____

_____

_____

_____

_____

_____

_____

_____

_____

_____

(Continue on your own paper.)

Revise the Draft

Use the chart below to help you revise your draft. Check YES or NO to answer each question in the chart. If you answer NO, make notes to remind yourself how you can revise, or change, your writing to improve it.

Question	YES ✔	NO ✔	If the answer is NO, what will you do to improve your writing?
Does your story describe a specific experience?			
Do you use descriptive language, or words that will help your readers see, hear, taste, feel, and smell?			
Do you use action words to describe what happens?			
Do you compare things in your story to other things to help readers imagine what you are describing?			
Do you organize the main ideas of your story into paragraphs?			
Do you use important details to support each main idea?			
Does your story have a beginning, middle, and end?			
Have you corrected mistakes in spelling, grammar, and punctuation?			

Use the notes in your chart and your writing plan to revise your draft.

Writing Report Card

Read your revised draft again or ask someone else to read it. Have the person who reads your paper complete the following Report Card. Revise your paper until you have no less than a Very Good Score for each item.

Title of paper: _____

Purpose of paper: _This is a descriptive story._____

_It describes something that happened to me._____

Person who scores the paper: _____

Score	Writing Goals
	Does the story describe a specific experience?
	Does the story have a strong beginning, or introduction?
	Does the story describe what the writer sees, hears, tastes, smells, and feels?
	Does the story have action words?
	Does the writer compare things to other things to help you imagine what he or she is describing?
	Are main ideas in the story presented in the order that they happened?
	Are there enough details to support each main idea?
	Is there a strong ending, or conclusion?
	Are the story's grammar, spelling, and punctuation correct?

☺ Excellent Score   ☆ Very Good Score   + Good Score
✔ Acceptable Score   − Needs Improvement

UNIT 6: Short Report

HOW MUCH DO YOU KNOW?

Read the short report. Answer the questions that follow.

Air, dust, and clouds make a blanket for the earth. This blanket helps protect us from the sun, but it is not enough. Ultraviolet rays, which are harmful and burning, still get through. Melanin is a substance in skin that gives some protection, but not everybody has enough of it. Melanin makes the skin darker, and it soaks up ultraviolet light.

If you tend to burn in the sun, you can make your own suntan lotion. This lotion can help protect light-skinned people from ultraviolet light. You mix oil and tea in a special way. Add the tea to the oil, then blend or beat until well mixed. Tea contains tannins that provide a sunscreen, and this mixture can block up to 50 percent of the sun's burning rays. This mixture will keep well in a bottle, but you must shake it well before using.

1. What would be a good title for this short report?

   _____

2. What is the topic of the first paragraph?

   _____

3. What is the topic of the second paragraph?

   _____

4. Which of these notes would be used to write this short report?

   _____

   a. Some of the best beaches in the United States are found in Florida.
   b. A lotion with an SPF of 30 provides 30 times your natural sunburn protection.
   c. Apply sunscreen generously and evenly to all exposed areas 30 minutes before sun exposure.
   d. Overexposure to the sun can cause premature skin aging, skin wrinkling, and skin cancer.

Analyzing a Short Report

A SHORT REPORT

- gives information about a topic
- draws facts from various sources
- has a title, an introduction, a body, and a conclusion

Read the short report. Answer the questions that follow.

Many of our superstitions came to us from very ancient sources. The idea that one should knock on wood for good luck, for example, is a 4,000-year-old custom that began with some Indian tribes of North America. Noticing that the oak was struck often by lightning, the Indians thought that it must be the dwelling place of a sky god. They also thought that boasting of a future personal deed was bad luck and meant the thing would never happen. Knocking on an oak tree was a way of contacting the sky god and being forgiven for boasting.

Another interesting superstition is that it is bad luck to open an umbrella indoors. In eighteenth-century England, umbrellas had stiff springs and very strong metal spokes. Opening one indoors could indeed cause an accident. It could injure someone or break a fragile object. This superstition came about for practical reasons.

1. What would be a good title for this short report?

   _____

2. What is the topic of the first paragraph?

   _____

3. What is the topic of the second paragraph?

   _____

4. What is one detail from the first paragraph?

   _____

Summarizing to Organize Notes

IN ORGANIZING NOTES FOR A SHORT REPORT, GOOD WRITERS

- use note cards and keep them organized
- summarize statements that have common ideas into one statement

A. Organize these note cards by writing the letter of the subject to which each one applies. Use these subjects: a. mountain heights; b. people who climbed mountains; c. special mountain-climbing words.

1. _____ Mount Roraima in South America is 9,092 feet high.

2. _____ Miriam O'Brien Underhill was the first woman to climb the Matterhorn, the Grepon, and other famous peaks without any help from men.

3. _____ Asia's Minya Konka is 24,900 feet high.

4. _____ Annapurna in Asia is 26,504 feet high.

5. _____ A *piton* is a metal spike used in mountain climbing to hold ropes in the side of the mountain.

6. _____ James W. Whitaker reached the top of Mt. Everest in 1963, along with Thomas F. Hombein, William F. Unsoeld, Luther G. Jerstad, and Barry C. Bishop.

7. _____ To *rappel* means to go down a cliff or a mountain, using a rope.

B. Read the group of note cards. Organize them into one note card.

8. a. In August 1980, Reinhold Messner climbed Mt. Everest alone.

    b. He was the first to climb Everest without any bottled oxygen.

    c. Messner did not even use a ladder or a rope.

    d. Messner carried no radio that might have kept him in touch with other people.

NEW CARD: _____

_____

Using Quotations

Good writers use quotations from oral and written sources.

Each numbered sentence below the box is the topic sentence of a paragraph in a short report about whales. The box contains sentences with quotations that might be used in the report. After each topic sentence, write the letter of the quotation sentence that should be included in that paragraph.

a. "These magnificent creatures are even larger than the famous dinosaurs that died out so long ago," commented Dr. Romley.

b. Dr. Schultz said, "Although international laws ban hunting, some species of whales are still in danger of extinction."

c. Mr. Walters explained, "The whale's nostrils, located on top of its head, can be tightly closed so that no water leaks in."

d. "I am still thrilled every time I hear these whales 'talking' to each other," said Mr. Clark.

e. "Though we often think of whales as huge animals," said Ms. Kwong, "some species are barely four feet long."

f. "A baleen whale has no teeth. Instead, it has thin plates, called baleen, in its mouth," added Mr. Walters.

1. A whale's body is specially adapted for its underwater life. _____

2. Whales vary greatly in size. _____

3. The blue whale is the largest animal that ever lived. _____

4. Whales make special sounds to communicate with each other and to navigate through the water. _____

5. Some species of whales have become endangered animals. _____

6. Baleen whales form one of the two major groups of whales. _____

Giving Your Sentences More Variety

> Good writers avoid using the same sentence pattern all the time.

Rewrite each sentence. Move a word or phrase to the beginning of the sentence so that it no longer starts with the sentence subject. You may have to reword other parts of the sentence, too.

1. Did you read about the Boston Tea Party for homework?

   _____

2. Patriots threw tea into Boston Harbor on December 16, 1773.

   _____

3. The tide was going out when the dumping occurred.

   _____

4. The chests were lined with lead.

   _____

5. They looked beautiful, painted with Chinese lacquer.

   _____

6. These were all simple wooden boxes, except for about 50 of the crates.

   _____

7. These 50 were large boxes of an ornate Chinese design.

   _____

8. An explorer plans to look for the boxes in Boston Harbor.

   _____

9. The tide has probably moved the chests farther out into the harbor.

   _____

Proofreading a Short Report

Proofread the beginning of the short report, paying special attention to capital letters in titles. Use the Proofreading Marks to correct at least eight errors.

PROOFREADING MARKS	
⬭	spell correctly
⊙	add period
?	add question mark
⹀	capitalize
℘	take out
∧	add
/	make lowercase
∿	switch
⩓	add comma
⌄ ⌄	add quotation marks
¶	indent paragraph

The Saltiest Lake in the World

The Dead Sea is the world's saltyest

body of water. Usually, sea water has a salt

content of 3.5 percent. The Dead sea is 28

percent salt, or eight times as salty as the

oceans. By comparison, the Great Salt Lake

in utah is six times as salty as Sea water. The water of the Dead Sea is so

salty that salt columns come up out of the water in strange formations.

Many people say these salt formations look like oddly formed, discolored

icebergs

the salt in the Dead Sea helped give the huge lake its name. The salt

in the water kills almost every form of life that is swept into the Dead Sea.

The salt is also the cause of the Dead Seas most well-known quality: its

buoyancy. According to Rupert o. Matthews in his book <u>The atlas of natural</u>

<u>Wonders</u>, "Sinking and diving are impossible, but it is far easier to swim

here than in any other stretch of water."

Write about Japanese Culture

With a friend, look up information on Japanese flower arranging (*ikebana*), dwarf trees (*bonsai*), or anything else about Japanese culture that interests you. Write a short report about what you learn.

_____

_____

_____

_____

_____

_____

_____

_____

_____

_____

_____

_____

_____

_____

_____

_____

Write about a Musical Figure

With a friend, choose a musical figure you both admire. Go to the library to read about him or her. You may wish to have the librarian show you how to find articles in magazines. List three quotations from the musician or about the musician. Write a report on the musician using the quotations in your report.

THREE QUOTATIONS:

_____

_____

_____

Interview Questions

Imagine that you and a friend have met a little baby who can talk. Write five questions you would ask the baby about his or her impressions of the world. Then write what the baby might say in answer to each of your questions.

Questions

1. _____

2. _____

3. _____

4. _____

5. _____

Baby Answers

1. _____

2. _____

3. _____

4. _____

5. _____

A Practice Short Report

LEFT-HANDED OR RIGHT-HANDED

You walk into a new class and see rows of empty desks. It's good that you're the first one here, because there's a problem. These aren't the big square desks you like best. These are what you call the half desks. The desks are made to let you slide into the seat. Then the desk sits under your arm. The problem is that all but one desk in the room is for right-handed people, and you're a leftie. You've done the math before. If there are thirty students in this class, at least three more people will want the same desk. It's a good thing you're here first.

This is a common problem. No one knows why more people are right-handed than left-handed. Scientists ask questions, but so far, they haven't found clear answers. There are a few things they do know. For example, if both parents are right-handed, then almost all of their children will be right-handed. If one of the parents is left-handed, the chances of having left-handed children go up. Now this might make you think that left-handed parents have left-handed children. But when both parents are left-handed, about half their children are right-handed. Puzzling, isn't it?

Some scientists report that 13 percent of people in the world are left-handed. Others report that as many as 30 percent of people are left-handed. There is a simple test you can do to determine which hand you use most. Sit comfortably and fold your hands together. Which thumb is on top? If you are right-handed, it's probably your left thumb. If you're left-handed, the thumb is reversed.

This test doesn't always work. You might want to ask yourself a few questions instead. For example, which hand do you use to do the following things?

- turn on the lights
- brush your teeth
- brush your hair
- pick up something from the ground
- throw a ball
- get your teacher's attention

Whichever answer you give most tells whether you're right-handed or left-handed.

Scientists aren't sure what causes people to use one hand more than the other. Some think that genes determine which hand we use more. Genes are the hereditary information we get from our parents. Some scientists explain that the gene for being right-handed is dominant. Dominant means that if you have this gene, you're right-handed. If you don't, you're left-handed. However, no scientist has found the gene. Plus, studies of identical twins tell us that genes may not be the answer. Identical twins have the same genes, but almost 20 percent of them have different handedness.

While some scientists try to find genes, other scientists look for different clues. Some scientists study how humans act and live. They have found tools made by people who lived during the Stone Age. Some of those tools are millions of years old. Some are only ten thousand years old. These tools tell scientists that the number of left-handed and right-handed people used to be about equal. Does this information leave you scratching your

FAMOUS LEFT-HANDED PEOPLE		
Historical Figures	Entertainers	Musicians
Alexander the Great	Charlie Chaplin	Ludwig van Beethoven
Julius Caesar	Marilyn Monroe	Ringo Starr
Napoleon Bonaparte	Oprah Winfrey	Paul McCartney
Athletes	Artists	Members of the British Royal Family
Monica Seles	Michelangelo	Queen Elizabeth II
Terry Labonte	Leonardo da Vinci	Prince Charles
Larry Bird	Pablo Picasso	Prince William

head? Which hand are you using? As you can see, scientists have more work to do.

Some people claim that most geniuses are left-handed. Benjamin Franklin was a leftie. So was Albert Einstein. So were Leonardo da Vinci and Michelangelo. One newspaper reported that one out of every three American presidents has been a leftie. There are plenty of famous lefties in the world. They work everywhere, including in science, art, music, and sports. Read the chart above to find a few familiar names.

Today there are fewer left-handed people than there are right-handed people. That means that it's hard for a leftie to find a pair of scissors or a desk. It's also hard to find bowling balls and boomerangs. However, things are changing. Lefties are speaking up. Now they have their own sports equipment and musical instruments. They have their own clubs and magazines. There's even an international holiday that celebrates lefties. Next year, you might want to join them.

Respond to the Practice Paper

Write your answers to the following questions or directions.

1. What is the problem in this report?

   _____

   _____

2. Why aren't scientists sure if genes are the reason we use one hand more than the other?

   _____

   _____

3. What have scientists learned about Stone Age people?

   _____

   _____

4. Write a paragraph to summarize this report. Use these questions to help you write your summary:
   - What is the report about?
   - What explanations does the writer give?
   - How is life changing for lefties?

   _____

   _____

   _____

   _____

   _____

   _____

   _____

Analyze the Practice Paper

Read "Left-Handed or Right-Handed" again. As you read, think about the main ideas the writer discusses. Write your answers to the following questions.

1. Read the first paragraph again. Why do you think the writer began the report this way?

    _____

    _____

2. Why do you think the writer ends the second paragraph with a question?

    _____

    _____

3. The writer uses some special words like *genes* and *dominant*. How does the writer make it easier for the reader to understand these words?

    _____

    _____

4. Why do you think the writer includes the work of scientists in this report?

    _____

    _____

5. Why is the last paragraph important? What makes it different from the other paragraphs?

    _____

    _____

    _____

    _____

Writing Assignment

In a short report, writers write about one topic, or subject. They research the topic to find important main ideas. They also find important details to support the main ideas. Write a short report about a science topic that interests you. Use this writing plan to help you write a first draft on the next page.

The topic of this paper is:

_____

Main Idea of Paragraph 1: _____

Detail: _____

Detail: _____

Detail: _____

Main Idea of Paragraph 2: _____

Detail: _____

Detail: _____

Detail: _____

Main Idea of Paragraph 3: _____

Detail: _____

Detail: _____

Detail: _____

First Draft

Use your writing plan as a guide as you write your first draft of a short report. Include a catchy title.

_____

_____

_____

_____

_____

_____

_____

_____

_____

_____

(Continue on your own paper.)

Revise the Draft

Use the chart below to help you revise your draft. Check YES or NO to answer each question in the chart. If you answer NO, make notes to remind yourself how you can revise, or change, your writing to improve it.

Question	YES ✔	NO ✔	If the answer is NO, what will you do to improve your writing?
Do you write about one science topic in your report?			
Do you introduce your topic in the first paragraph?			
Do you have more than one main idea?			
Do you organize your main ideas into paragraphs?			
Do you include details to support each main idea?			
Do you summarize your report in the last paragraph?			
Have you corrected mistakes in spelling, grammar, and punctuation?			

Use the notes in your chart and your writing plan to revise your draft.

Writing Report Card

Read your revised draft again or ask someone else to read it. Have the person who reads your paper complete the following Report Card. Revise your paper until you have no less than a Very Good Score for each item.

Title of paper: _____

Purpose of paper: _*This is a short report.*_____

Person who scores the paper: _____

Score	Writing Goals
	Is this paper an example of a short report?
	Does the writer talk about a specific topic, or subject?
	Does the report introduce the topic in the first paragraph?
	Does the report have more than one main idea?
	Are the main ideas organized into paragraphs?
	Does the way the paragraphs are organized make sense?
	Are there details to support each main idea?
	Does the writer summarize the report in the last paragraph?
	Does the writer "stick" to the topic throughout the report?
	Are the report's grammar, spelling, and punctuation correct?

☺ Excellent Score   ☆ Very Good Score   + Good Score
✔ Acceptable Score   – Needs Improvement

Answer Key

Answers to the practice paper exercises questions may vary, but examples are provided here to give you an idea of how your child may respond.

Unit 1: Personal Narrative

p. 6
Possible responses: 1. Susie's sister
2. the preparations for the party 3. She was surprised and happy. 4. They wore polka-dot party hats, ate, laughed, danced.

p. 7
Possible responses: 1. what happens when the writer gets a Mohawk haircut 2. getting the haircut 3. the reaction of his mother 4. the reaction of his teacher 5. what happens during the school play

p. 8
1. none 2. cause: Two grizzly bears suddenly appeared, effect: The men were immediately frightened. 3. cause: The men fired, effect: One bear was wounded. 4. cause: The other bear was not hurt, effect: It ran away. 5. cause: The wounded bear was very angry, effect: It charged Captain Lewis. 6. cause: Because Lewis still had time to reload, effect: He lived to tell the tale. 7. none 8. cause: If you bother or frighten a grizzly, effect: It will attack. 9. cause: It goes its own way, effect: A person avoids trouble. 10. cause: Because these bears do not climb trees, effect: Many people have escaped angry grizzlies.

p. 9
1. He had a slow and serious nature. 2. He was already an expert rider. 3. The Crow Indians had stolen some Sioux horses. 4. It was considered braver to push an enemy off a horse than to shoot an arrow from far away. 5. Slow had jabbed the Crow with his stick. 6. They had won the battle.

p. 10
Be sure that answers are synonyms for the underlined words. Possible responses:
1. huge 2. approximately 3. raising
4. labored diligently 5. farmed 6. The situation; difficult 7. stores 8. enterprising 9. Three decades; nation 10, 11, 12. Responses will vary. Be sure that synonyms are vivid.

p. 11–12
Last weekend I traveled more than a
hundred
(hunderd) years back in time. No, I didn't

find a time machine—I went to the Dickens

Fair in San Francisco. The (fare) was held
fair

on Pier 45 at the (famuos) Fisherman's
famous

Wharf. The whole wharf was crowded with

people, and everyone seemed to be having
great
a (grate) time!

The people who worked at the Dickens Fair

were all dressed the way people dressed in
England
(Engaland) when Charles Dickens was

alive. The women wore long dresses, and

most of the men had fancy hats. These

people all spoke with English accents and

used special phrases. My parents especially

liked being greeted by people who said,

"Hello fair lady" and "Good day, kind sir."

there were some special booths at the
hours
dickens Fair. My older sister spent (ours)
jewelry
looking at the (jewlry.) Finally, she chose a
pair
(pare) of earrings. I had fun looking at all the
buy
booths, but I didn't (by) anything.

p. 20
1. Benny wrote "The Mysterious Atlantic Ocean Fish" to tell his story in his own words and to explain how he became friends with Sammy. The very first sentence says, "I'm Benny, and here's my story." 2. Benny begins by explaining why he doesn't want to be friends with Sammy. He says Sammy is too young to be included in games with his other friends. 3. Benny says that he and Sammy have grown close. He goes on to say that they like to trade books and play video games together. 4. Be sure your child correctly summarizes the significant events of the story, paraphrasing as needed.

p. 21
1. Benny uses words such as *I, me,* and *my* to show that he is writing about his personal experiences. 2. A younger kid, Sammy, lives across the hall and wants to be Benny's friend. Benny thinks Sammy is too young to be his friend. Then Benny's dad invites Sammy to the beach. With Benny's help, Sammy brings home an ocean fish. Sammy asks Benny for help when the fish gets sick.

3. Benny adds fresh water to the fish bowl. He saves the fish, and in the process, he and Sammy become friends. 4. Benny shares his funny inner thoughts with us by talking directly to us. When the fish gets sick, he says something really funny: "I start making funeral plans." Also, Benny keeps our interest by telling us about the fish. We want to find out what happens to it. 5. In the first paragraph, Benny tells us why he and Sammy cannot be friends and why he doesn't want to introduce Sammy to his other friends. In the last paragraph, Benny ties up the loose ends of the story and tells us that he and Sammy are now friends and that they play ball with Benny's friends.

Unit 2: How-to Writing

p. 20
Time-order words and phrases may vary. First, pick out your favorite color of balloon. Stretch the balloon several times. Then, blow it up slowly. The next thing you do is tie a knot in the balloon. Then, tie a ribbon around the knot. Last, hang it from the ribbon. 1. how to blow up a balloon 2. Pick out your favorite color of balloon.

p. 27
1. two items—a microwave oven and popcorn 2. Take the plastic overwrap off and place the bag in the microwave. 3. Set the timer and start the microwave. 4. Stop the microwave when the popping slows down. 5. Remove the bag from the microwave and shake it.

p. 28
Time-order words and phrases may vary. To wash your family car, there are six steps you should follow. First, get a bucket. Then, fill the bucket with soapy water. Next, hose down the car to get it wet. After that, wash the car, using the soapy water and a soft cloth or sponge. The next thing you do is dry the car. Finally, shine the windows and any chrome trim.

p. 29
Possible responses: 1. the first one—It gives very detailed directions, as if this were the first time the reader had ever chopped an onion. 2. the second one—It assumes that the reader has done this before; and therefore, it leaves out some of the details. 3. how to peel the onion; directions on being very careful not to cut fingers; an explanation of what a cutting board is; more explanation of what "lengthwise" and "crosswise" mean

p. 30
1. a. You'll need 101 index cards. You'll need a colored marker. b. You'll need 101 index

cards, and you'll need a colored marker.
2. a. Print the name of a state or a state capital on each index card. Print the rules on the last index card. b. Print the name of a state or a state capital on each index card, and print the rules on the last index card. 3. a. Put the marker away. Put all the cards in an envelope. b. Put the marker away, and put all the cards in an envelope. 4. a. This game is for small groups. Up to three students may play. b. This game is for small groups, and up to three students may play. 5. a. Players mix up the cards. They lay the cards face down. b. Players mix up the cards, and they lay the cards face down.

p. 31–32

Do you have a little brother or sister?

Do you sometimes help take care of little children? If so, you might want to make a set of special building blocks. These blocks are large and light enough for even a two-year-old to handle *easily.* They are sturdy and colorful, and they can be lots of fun.

To make a set of blocks, you need as many half-gallon milk cartons *as* you can collect. you also need sheets of colorful paper and some glue.

For each block, use two of your milk cartons. Cut the tops off both cartons. Then wash them thoroughly and let them dry. Be sure your cartons are completely clean.

When both cartons are dry, push the open end of one *carton* into the other carton. Press the two cartons together as far as possible. You should end up with a block that is the size of a single carton, with both ends closed and with extra-long sides. Then cover each block, using glue and the paper you have chosen.

p. 40

1. This how-to paper teaches you how to decorate a T-shirt. 2. The materials needed to decorate a T-shirt include 1 white T-shirt, an 8 in. x 8 in. piece of drawing paper, pen or pencil, 2 safety pins, transfer paper, and 3 or 4 felt-tipped pens in different colors. 3. The first thing to think about is where to wear the T-shirt. 4. The second thing to think about is what to put on the T-shirt. 5. The third thing to think about is the T-shirt's colors. 6. Answers will vary, but look for indications of understanding, such as a clear description of the T-shirt and a corresponding illustration.

p. 41

1. The writer states the purpose of the paper clearly, lists materials, gives clear step-by-step instructions, and gives helpful hints and details. 2. Sequence words such as now, first, and second help the reader understand the order of the steps. 3. The writer lists the materials so they can be collected before starting the project. That saves time and makes the project easier to do. 4. The numbered steps make the complicated process easier to understand. It shows that each step builds on a previous step and that each needs to be done in order. 5. Pictures and answers may vary. Check pictures to determine if your child understood the instructions.

Unit 3: Story

p. 46

1. Paul Bunyan and Juan 2. They discuss solving the problem of cold food in the big dining hall. 3. a. He is Paul Bunyan's helper. b. He is smaller than Paul.

p. 47–48

1. the wife, the husband, and the baby
2. their home and field 3. A husband who thinks his wife can't do anything right trades jobs with her. 4. The husband and the wife agree to trade jobs. 5. The baby's diaper ends up on the baby's head.

p. 49

Possible responses: 1. a. "You know I'll be sure to do it later." b. "This is the best time of day for a swim." 2. a. Sal ran out, wearing his bathing suit. b. After his swim, Sal fell asleep. 3. a. "He's always into some mischief, but I know he's a good boy deep down." b. "Where are you going in such a hurry. You know you have chores to do."

p. 50

Possible responses: 1. Gabrielle had a bad toothache on the right side of her mouth. 2. Her mother drove her to the dentist's office on the other side of town. 3. Gabrielle did not have to wait for very long. 4. The dentist's assistant had her sit in the big chair in the first room. 5. The assistant took an X-ray of Gabrielle's mouth. 6. The dentist looked at the X-ray on the light table.

p. 51–52

One of Paul Bunyan's helpers stared up at Paul and shook his head. "How will we ever get all this hot food *to* two the tables?" he asked. The dining hall is so big that the food gets cold before we can serve it. "Why, that's easy," answered Paul. " We'll just put roller skates on the ponies. Then the ponies can skate in quickly and deliver the food before it gets cold." "What a great idea!" cried Paul Bunyan's helpers. The next night, however, Paul and his helpers discovered that his idea wasn't great after all. The ponies weren't good roller-skaters. They spilled most of the food, and then they stopped to eat the spilled food. "What a mess!" exclaimed Paul. "What will we do?" asked his helpers.

"Well," said Paul, "first, we'll have to clean up the dining hall. Then, I think we should build tracks between the *rows* rose of tables. We can use freight trains to deliver the food."

p. 59

1. Tanisha and Jemma live in a future time when students take field trips to Mars and have clones. Also, kids play in anti-gravity chambers and can download experiences from and into their clones. 2. In the beginning of the story, Tanisha is helping Jemma put on her leg brace. Later, Jemma smooths her school uniform. These are clues that the girls are in Jemma's bedroom getting ready for school. Other clues in the story, such as the clone, suggest that the time is in the future. 3. Jemma hurt her leg in the anti-gravity chamber and won't be able to pass her physical fitness test. If she doesn't take and pass the test, she won't be able to go on the class trip to Mars. 4. Tanisha suggests that Jemma let her clone practice for the physical fitness test. Then Jemma can download the experience. 5. Be sure that your child correctly summarizes the significant events of the story, paraphrasing as needed.

p. 60

1. The writer uses dialogue to make the story seem like a typical school day for two good friends. 2. The writer includes fantastic details about the future. There is an anti-gravity chamber, a class trip to Mars, and clones that

can go to school with their owners. 3. The writer uses dialogue to make the unbelievable seem believable. The story is told through a conversation between the girls. 4. The mood of the story is playful. First, Tanisha teases Jemma about playing in the anti-gravity chamber. Both girls laugh about the time Jemma sent her clone to take her French test and the clone had a meltdown and caught on fire. Finally, Tanisha teases Jemma again, saying that if the clone passes the fitness test, the clone can go on the school trip.

Unit 4: Comparative Writing

p. 65
1. The first time LeAnn went to visit her friend Vanessa, she noticed how much Vanessa's furniture was like her own. 2. both are made of pine, both were chosen by an aunt 3. one is a rolltop and one has a flat surface.

p. 66
1. the Tasady and the Ik tribes 2. Neither tribe knew about the outside world until recently, both still live in the Stone Age, both live in the mountains. 3. The Tasady live in caves, and the Ik live in grass huts. The Tasady have plenty of food, but the Ik do not. The Tasady have a good chance of surviving, but the Ik may not. 4. contrasts

p. 67
Responses will vary. Be sure that likenesses and differences are appropriate.

p. 68
1. formal 2. informal 3. informal 4. formal 5. formal 6. informal 7. formal 8. formal 9. formal 10. informal 11. formal

p. 69
1. The Pygmies live in the forest in Africa, and they hunt there. 2. Pygmy men are about four and a half feet tall, and the women are even smaller. 3. They are the smallest people in the world, and their small size helps them to hide. 4. Children the same age call boys "brother," and they call girls "sister." 5. Pygmies look at a broken branch, and they can tell which animal has been there. 6. Pygmies know a lot about plants, and they can tell which are good to eat.

p. 70–71
The first time Lee went to visit his friend Vladimir, he noticed how much Vlad's furniture was like his own. He saw that the desk in Vlad's room was made of pine, just like Lee's desk. Vlad's mom had chosen the desk, just as lee's mom had chosen Lee's. Lee also noticed the bed in Vlad's room.

Vlad explained that it had been his grandfather's bed. Lee remembered that the bed in his own room had once belonged to his dad's dad.

As Lee looked at Vlad's bed, he pictured his own bed in his mind. Lee's bed was made of brass and steel. It had been made in England more then (than) 100 years ago. Vlad's desk, on the other hand, was dark wood with a tall hedboard (headboard). It had been made in Russia about 60 years ago. Lee realized that he would rather have a bed like Vlad's. The headboard was good for holding books.

p. 78
Guide your child in organizing the information in a clear manner. How American Black Bears and Polar Bears Are Alike: Both are large, smart bears.; Both can be found in Canada.; Both have heavy fur coats.; Both have a good sense of smell.; Both use their sense of smell to find food.; Both eat small animals.; Both sometimes eat dead animals.; Both hibernate.; Both have young that are born blind.; Both commonly give birth to twins.; Both have young that grow quickly.; Both are endangered.; Both are models for stuffed toy bears.
How American Black Bears and Polar Bears Are Different: American black bears live in most of the United States; polar bears live along the coasts of Canada, Greenland, and Siberia, and on islands in the Arctic Ocean.; American black bears live in forests; polar bears live where there is ice.; The adult male black bear is between 3 and 4 feet tall and weighs between 135 and 350 lbs.; the adult male polar bear stands 8 to 11 feet tall and weighs more than 1,000 lbs.; Black bears like berries, nuts, grass, and other plants; polar bears are meat-eaters that feed mainly on seals.; Black bears are chocolate brown, cinnamon, blond, and silver gray; polar bears have fur that looks white or yellow.; Black bears hibernate in the winter; only pregnant female polar bears hibernate.; Black bears are usually born in January or February; polar bears are often born in December.; Black bear cubs weigh less than 1 pound at birth; new born polar bear cubs weigh $1\frac{1}{2}$ pounds.

p. 79
1. The writer gets our attention by linking the subject of the paper to something we know

and love, namely, teddy bears. 2. The writer tells us a story about how President Roosevelt's meeting with a real bear ended and how teddy bears were named as a result. 3. The color of the bears' fur is discussed. 4. The writer uses the bears' powerful sense of smell to introduce the topic of what bears eat. 5. In the last paragraph, the writer summarizes how American black bears and polar bears are alike. The writer ties the last paragraph to the first paragraph by saying that both kinds of bears are "wonderful models for the stuffed bears we love so much."

Unit 5: Descriptive Writing

p. 85
1. a box turtle 2. a. hinged lower shell b. can pull its legs, head, and tail inside its shell c. eats earthworms, insects, berries, and green leafy vegetables 3. smooth–touch, hard–touch 4. rustle–hearing, loud–hearing

p. 86, 87
1. Thanksgiving 2. Thanksgiving has to be my favorite holiday. 3. a. aromas of turkey roasting and pumpkin pies baking b. autumn colors of orange, gold, red, and brown flowers c. the sound of children laughing and music playing 4. a kitchen just before a special feast 5. Did you ever walk into the kitchen of a good cook just before a special feast?

p. 88
A.1. left to right 2. top to bottom
B. Responses will vary. Be sure that the organization is appropriate.

p. 89
1. blue–sight; suit–sight 2. cool–touch; water–sight 3. large–sight; black–sight 4. loud–hearing 5. hair–sight; chlorine–smell 6. rough–touch, sight; jagged–touch, sight 7. foot–sight, touch; yelled–hearing 8. soft–touch, sight; bandage–sight, touch 9. warm–touch; soft–touch 10. delicious–taste; sandwich–taste, sight, smell

p. 90
Possible responses: 1. Young Soren rolled in the grass under a tree and watched the sailboats. 2. The ships were going to Baltimore or sailing out to sea. 3. Young Soren did not know what geography and arithmetic books were. 4. He had never been to school or learned how to read. 5. The hill was a good place to stand and watch the boats. 6. Soren visited his grandmother in the summer and his uncle in the winter.

p. 91–92
Aunt jane (Jane) said she would have a surprise for us last saturday (Saturday), but she refused to give us any hints. Just after breakfast, we heard a low humming sound in our driveway. It was

followed by an unusual, squeaky car horn. ‸A

car! A car!" my ~~S~~ister shouted. "Aunt Jane's

surprise is a ¢ar!"

We all rushed out to see Aunt Jane's

new car, and what a surprise it was! Her

"new" car was more than 50 years old. It

was a beautiful 1938 whippet. Its bright

green surface shimmered in the sunlight. Its

long hood stretched forward elegantly, and

its whitewall tires gleamed on our dusty

driveway⊙

"Oh, jane," said mom. "What a great car!

May we get in?"

"Of course," laughed Aunt Jane, and she

clicked the front door open for us. The inside

of the car was dark and cool and filled with

the soft smell of old ⟨lether.⟩ *leather*

"Let's go for a drive," suggested dad. "Who

wants to ride out to Lake barton?"

p. 100
1. The writer describes the Gonzalez family's "vacation" experience at a museum. 2. Everyone in the family wants to go to a different place on the family vacation. 3. Miguel wants to see the ocean. Angela wants to visit the White House. Mrs. Gonzalez wants to go to Arizona to see a rodeo. Mr. Gonzalez wants to visit Yellowstone National Park. 4. Mrs. Gonzalez solves her family's problem by taking them to a museum where they can see paintings of all the places they want to go. 5. Be sure that your child correctly summarizes the significant events of the story, paraphrasing as needed.

p. 101
1. The writer uses descriptive action words, such as "soared," "swooped," "squirming," "gripped," "steaming," and "shimmered." 2. The writer uses descriptive phrases, such as "blue-green water looked as smooth as silk," "a net filled with slick, squirming fish," and "the White House shimmered in the light." 3. Possible answer: The seagulls' feathers combed through the strands of fiery sunlight like soft, white fingers. 4. Possible answer: The spouting geyser made a mighty mountain of steam and water. 5. Another surprise ending might be that Mrs. Gonzalez entered a travel contest on the Internet and won! The grand prize was an all-expense-paid family trip around the United States.

Unit 6: Short Report

p. 106
Possible responses:
1. Protection from Ultraviolet Rays 2. how ultraviolet rays are harmful 3. how to make your own suntan lotion 4. b, c, d

p. 107
Possible responses: 1. Some Superstitions and Their Origins 2. knocking on wood for good luck 3. opening umbrellas indoors is bad luck 4. Response should include one of the following: The custom is four thousand years old. The Indians thought the oak was the dwelling place of a sky god. They thought that knocking on an oak tree was a way of contacting the sky god and being forgiven for boasting.

p. 108
1. a 2. b 3. a 4. a 5. c 6. b 7. c 8. In 1980 Reinhold Messner climbed Mt. Everest alone, without bottled oxygen, a ladder, a rope, or a radio.

p. 109
1. c 2. e 3. a 4. d 5. b 6. f

p. 110
Possible responses: 1. For homework, did you read about the Boston Tea Party? 2. On December 16, 1773, patriots threw tea into Boston Harbor. 3. When the dumping occurred, the tide was going out. 4. Lead lined the chests. 5. Painted with Chinese lacquer, they looked beautiful. 6. Except for about 50 of the crates, these were all simple wooden boxes. 7. Of an ornate Chinese design, these 50 were large boxes. 8. In Boston Harbor an explorer plans to look for the boxes. 9. Probably the tide has moved the chests farther out into the harbor.

p. 111–112
The Dead Sea is the world's ⟨saltyest⟩ *saltiest*

body of water. Usually, sea water has a salt

content of 3.5 percent. The Dead sea is 28

percent salt, or eight times as salty as the

oceans. By comparison, the Great Salt Lake

in utah is six times as salty as ~~S~~ea water.

The water of the Dead Sea is so salty that

salt columns come up out of the water in

strange formations. Many people say these

salt formations look like oddly formed,

discolored icebergs⊙

the salt in the Dead Sea helped give the

huge lake its name. The salt in the water

kills almost every form of life that is swept

into the Dead Sea. The salt is also the

cause of the Dead Sea‸s most well-known

quality: its buoyancy. According to Rupert o.

Matthews in his book The atlas of natural

Wonders, "Sinking and diving are

impossible, but it is far easier to swim here

than in any other stretch of water."

p. 119
1. The problem is that there aren't enough left-handed desks or other specially designed items available to left-handers. 2. Scientists are not sure if left-handedness relates to genes because research shows that if both parents are left-handed, about half of their children are right-handed. Also, identical twins have the same genes, but almost 20 percent of them have different handedness. 3. Tools made by Stone Age people show scientists that the number of left-handed and right-handed people used to be about equal. 4. Be sure that your child identifies the report's main ideas and include significant details.

p. 120
1. The writer gives an example of what it is like to be left-handed in a right-handed world. This example makes us want to read more. 2. The writer includes the reader in the puzzle and grabs the reader's attention by asking that short question. 3. The writer uses simpler words to define each word that the reader might not know. 4. The writer includes facts from scientists' work to show that he or she did research for this report. The facts also give interesting information about the kinds of questions scientists are asking, what they know, and what they don't know. 5. The last paragraph repeats the subject of the first paragraph. That helps tie the beginning of the report to the ending. The conclusion also brings the reader into the report. The writer says, "Next year you might want to join them."